LONDON VILLAGES

LONDON VILLAGES

ZENA ALKAYAT

WITH
PHOTOGRAPHS BY KIM LIGHTBODY
& ILLUSTRATED MAPS BY JENNY SEDDON

FRANCES LINCOLN LIMITED
PUBLISHERS

London Villages

CONTENTS

INTRODUCTION

London is often described as a series of 'villages'. This rather romantic image is partly down to history (the capital grew by consuming the constellation of communities that surrounded it), and partly because Londoners have long found ways to make this vast, intense city feel a more intimate and manageable place to live.

In reality, London firmly remains one sprawling metropolis, and this book doesn't mean to pretend otherwise. Instead, it hopes to introduce visitors and locals to enclaves within the city that have a distinct character, sparky community spirit and keen sense of localism. These may be ancient villages (Hampstead, for example, was in the Domesday Book), or more simply a picturesque spot with typical village-like features – a farmers' market, say, or a pretty central green. It also homes in on streets and locations that have recently developed into contemporary urban 'villages' by virtue of a thriving medley of independent businesses, from butchers and bakers to cafés and boutiques.

There's space here for just thirty of these destinations: a geographically diverse mix of iconic London villages and little-known neighbourhoods. By celebrating the essence of each and revealing local highlights, this book hopes to inspire both Londoners and visitors to take an alternative approach to exploring this incredible city.

CENTRAL

MARYLEBONE VILLAGE

Marylebone has always been a well-to-do area, but the 1990s saw it become something of a fashionable destination. Smart boutiques began to open along its central spine, Marylebone High Street, and several upmarket restaurants soon followed suit. Today, the road is crammed with chic fashion labels (Whistles, The Kooples), aspirational homeware stores (Conran Shop, Skandium), appealing charity shops and excellent pubs and cafés. It's quite rightly regarded as a more interesting shopping alternative to the more mainstream Oxford Street to the south, and though the invariably wealthy residents see it as their village, it has none of the stiffness of London's more po-faced moneyed areas. This lack of pretension is in part to do with its West End location, which ensures stray tourists and Londoners from further afield make as much use of it as the locals. Those who venture beyond the busy main high street will also find more specialist businesses quietly thriving. Chiltern Street, for example, hides a run of bridal shops, as well as woodwind instrument makers Howarth and Cadenhead's Whisky Shop and Tasting Room. On Moxon Street, let your nose lead you to La Fromagerie cheese shop, while Marylebone Lane is home to ribbon specialist VV Rouleaux.

1 DAUNT BOOKS

83 Marylebone High St, W1U 4QW
☎ 7224 2295 🖳 www.dauntbooks.co.uk
9am-7.30pm Mon-Sat; 11am-6pm Sun

One of London's most prized bookshops, Daunt is loved as much for its Edwardian charm as for its superbly curated fiction, non-fiction and children's book collections. True to its origins as a travel bookshop, it continues to arrange guides and literature by country in a grand backroom and along its oak mezzanine.

2 MARYLEBONE FARMERS' MARKET

Cramer Street Car Park, W1U 4EW
🖥 www.lfm.org.uk
10am-2pm Sun

Despite being one of London's largest farmers' markets, this weekly event, held in a car park behind the high street, is easy to miss. Locals tend to keep it a secret, but follow the ladies wielding wicker baskets and they'll lead you to some forty stalls selling farm produce, artisan preserves, hot food and wines.

3 THE WALLACE COLLECTION

Hertford House, Manchester Square,
W1U 3BN ☎ 7563 9500
🖥 www.wallacecollection.org
10am-5pm Mon-Sun

This exceptional collection of art, decorative items, furniture and firearms amassed between 1760 and 1880 is displayed in the opulent rooms of the seventeenth-century Hertford House. A visit to the free museum should be coupled with a meal at its elegant courtyard restaurant.

4 PAUL ROTHE & SON

35 Marylebone Lane, W1U 2NN
☎ 7935 6783
🖥 www.paulrotheandsondelicatessen.co.uk
8am-6pm Mon-Fri; 11.30am-5.30pm Sat

Rows of jams and condiments line the windows and walls of this family-run café, which started life as a German deli in 1900. Pop in to browse the shelves, or settle on bolted-down chairs and tables for tea, sandwiches and a bit of banter with Paul Rothe, grandson of the original founder.

5 THE BUTTON QUEEN

76 Marylebone Lane, W1U 2PR
☎ 7935 1505
🖥 www.thebuttonqueen.co.uk
10am-5.30pm Mon-Fri; 10am-3pm Sat

Whether you're looking for an elusive button, or you're merely after a bit of inspiration for a craft project, this cute shop can help. Hundreds of vintage and new fasteners are arranged in folders and boxes, and the owners offer button covering and sourcing services.

POPCORN

CURZON STREET

TREBECK STREET

③ ②

SHEPHERD MARKET

YE Grapes 1882

④

MARKET MEWS

⑤

SHEPHERD STREET

WHITE HORSE STREET

GREEN PARK

HERTFORD STREET

①

Shepherd Market

BRICK STREET

PICCADILLY

GREEN PARK

HYDE PARK CORNER

SHEPHERD MARKET

Laid out by architect Edward Shepherd in 1735, the secluded streets of Mayfair's Shepherd Market have been privy to some salacious goings-on over the centuries, and a slightly seedy atmosphere still lingers in its narrow network of passageways. The village's historic associations with prostitution, however, are muted by its central location (penned in by the well-heeled Curzon Street and boisterous Piccadilly) and its attractive chocolate-box façade.

Behind the picturesque shopfronts lie an array of chichi boutiques, and longstanding services include a cobbler, pharmacy and builders' merchant. The village's main appeal, though, is drinking and dining. High-end restaurants spill alfresco into the alleyways, and a number of popular pubs and bars (including celeb hangout and members' club 5 Hertford Street) give Shepherd Market a lively personality come evening. The raucous mood gently recalls the annual two-week long May Fair, when crowds would descend on the site for a spot of revelry, gambling and drinking. The event was deemed an affront to public decency and banned in the early eighteenth century, and the area has continued in its attempts to cultivate a refined image ever since.

1 GEO. F. TRUMPER

9 Curzon St, W1J 5HQ
☎ *7499 1850* ▦ *www.trumpers.com*
9am-5.30pm Mon-Fri; 9am-5pm Sat
Groomed gents have been enjoying a
little primp and preen at this elegant
barbershop since 1875, and its dark
mahogany interior, private cubicles and
traditional wet shave service have barely
changed over the decades.

2 ANDERSON WHEELER

13 Shepherd Market, W1J 7PQ
☎ *7499 9315*
▦ *www.andersonwheeler.co.uk*
10am-6pm Mon-Fri
What might be an unusual sight on most
high streets – a bespoke gun and rifle
makers – looks right at home nestled
among the crooked lanes of Shepherd
Market. Hunting jackets, cartridge bags and
shooting binoculars can be found upstairs,
while the basement gunroom houses
impressive hand-crafted firearms.

③ LE BOUDIN BLANC

5 Trebeck St, W1J 7LT
☎ *7499 3292* 🖥 *www.boudinblanc.co.uk*
Noon-3pm & 6pm-11pm Mon-Sat;
noon-3pm & 6pm-10.30pm Sun

Classic French cuisine, a connoisseur's wine list and rowdy regulars mean this Gallic favourite is always abuzz. Try for a seat outside in fine weather: you'll feel like you're lunching in a Parisian courtyard.

④ CURZON MAYFAIR

38 Curzon St, W1J 7TY ☎ *0330 500 1331*
🖥 *www.curzoncinemas.com*

First opened in 1934 (though demolished and rebuilt in the 1960s), the Curzon Mayfair is a long-serving bastion of foreign and arthouse film, and was one of the first cinemas in the UK to import international movies.

⑤ SHEPHERDS TAVERN

50 Hertford St, W1J 7SS
☎ *7499 3017* 🖥 *www.taylor-walker.co.uk*
11am-11pm Mon-Sat; noon-10.30pm Sun

While this village is known for its Victorian boozers (Ye Grapes at 16 Shepherd Market is a favourite), Shepherds Tavern predates them by some way. Its doors opened in 1735, just as architect Edward Shepherd was initially developing the area.

PORCHESTER PLACE

EDGWARE ROAD

HYDE PARK CRESCENT

OXFORD SQUARE

5

COCOMAMA

2 1 4
3 CONNAUGHT STREET

CONNAUGHT SQUARE

ALBION STREET

PORTSEA PLACE

Connaught
Village

MARBLE
ARCH

BAYSWATER ROAD

HYDE PARK

CONNAUGHT VILLAGE

Edgware Road, with its spirited Middle Eastern community and horn-blaring traffic, tends to do a good job of keeping the sleepy Connaught Village under wraps. Make your way in via the south end of Edgware Road: you'll know you're close when you spy the grand stucco houses of the area's affluent residents, or spot the armed guards that protect the home of Tony Blair and his family on Connaught Square. Like other parts of this Paddington locale, the square follows the formal designs of English architect Samuel Pepys Cockerell who was initially involved in giving the area (then known as Tyburnia) a facelift in the early nineteenth century. It was a time of ambitious and costly rejuvenation that went some way toward eclipsing Tyburnia's more macabre history as the site of Tyburn Tree – an infamous gallows which saw plenty of use between 1196 and 1783. A model of the scaffold can be seen in the crypt at Tyburn Convent, a beautiful central London monastery whose Benedictine nuns have kept relics of the Catholic martyrs that were hanged nearby. The convent's address is 8-9 Hyde Park Place, though its entrance is actually on Bayswater Road overlooking the 350-acre royal Hyde Park.

① COCOMAYA

3 Porchester Place, W2 2BS
☎ *7706 2770 ▦ www.cocomaya.co.uk*
Bakery: 7am-7pm Mon-Fri; 8am-7pm
Sat; 8am-6pm Sun. Chocolatier:
10am-7pm Mon-Sat; 11am-6pm Sun
The sweet-toothed can browse and buy
creative chocs (shaped like skulls, for
example, or flavoured with lavender)
in Cocomaya's seductive boudoir-style
chocolatier, before heading to its light-
drenched bakery next door for divine
pastries, tarts and cakes. Each shop
has a large communal table.

② ATELIER MAYER

47 Kendal St, W2 2BU
☎ *7706 7200*
▦ *www.atelier-mayer.com*
10am-6pm Mon-Sat
(ideally by appointment)
Atelier Mayer may look closed, but ring
the doorbell and you'll be let into a
wonderland of designer vintage clothing
across two floors. Founder Carman Haid
has a sharp eye for occasionwear, and an
in-store appointment may well reward you
with a super-luxe gown by the likes
of Givenchy or Lanvin.

③ WILLIAM MANSELL

24 Connaught St, W2 2AF
☎ *7723 4154* 🖥 *www.williammansell.co.uk*
9.30am-5pm Mon-Fri

William Mansell has been tackling tricky watch and clock repairs for more than 145 years, and the creaky old store appears to be frozen in time. If you don't have a ticker in need of restoration, pop in to browse new and antique timepieces and jewellery.

④ DE ROEMER

114 Porchester Place, W2 2BS
☎ *3463 1971* 🖥 *www.deroemer.com*
10.30am-6.30pm Mon-Sat

You'll need a sturdy credit limit if you fancy going wild in the aisles of this contemporary cashmere store. But Tamsin De Roemer's line of easy-to-wear jumpers, T-shirts and dresses are worth investing in, as are the designer's butter-soft leather bags and fashionable collection of fine jewellery.

⑤ ST JOHN'S HYDE PARK

Hyde Park Crescent, W2 2QD
☎ *7262 1732* 🖥 *www.stjohns-hydepark.com*

This central London church attracts an enthusiastic congregation on Sunday mornings, particularly so on Horseman's Sunday. This annual September event sees the vicar mount a horse, invite churchgoers to do the same, and celebrate equestrianism in the city by blessing the animals and leading a family-friendly cavalcade and fair. The spectacle harks back to 1968 when riders took to their steeds to protest against the closure of the area's stables.

RUSSELL
SQUARE

CORAM'S
FIELDS

1

GUILFORD STREET

2

MILLMAN STREET

Charles Dickens
museum

JOHN STREET

GREAT ORMOND STREET

LAMB'S CONDUIT STREET

3

RUGBY STREET

5

4

East
Bloomsbury

THEOBALDS ROAD

GRAY'S INN
GARDENS

HOLBORN

EAST BLOOMSBURY

Lamb's Conduit Street has been the backbone of this mini-neighbourhood since the early 1800s when many of the street's houses were taken over by shopkeepers responding to a local demand for retail. Today it remains pleasantly removed from the main tourist trail that swings past the British Museum, and provides another excuse to visit an area primarily associated with the Bloomsbury Group. This artsy, intellectual set – including John Maynard Keynes and Virginia Woolf – haven't been Bloomsbury's only residents of distinction: Charles Dickens lived at 48 Doughty Street (now the Dickens Museum) and Charles Darwin resided in Gower Street. Sylvia Plath and Ted Hughes were said to enjoy a drink at The Lamb, and the pub (at the top of Lamb's Conduit Street) is a good place to take a break while exploring the road's flurry of cool boutiques. The surrounding streets are equally worth rambling around, offering up coffee shops such as The Espresso Room (31-35 Great Ormond Street), a huddle of gift shops on Rugby Street and secret patches of green nestled among the buildings. Make particular note of Gray's Inn Gardens to the south, which was laid out by Sir Francis Bacon in 1606.

1 CORAM'S FIELDS

93 Guilford St, WC1N 1DN
☎ 7837 6138 ⌨ www.coramsfields.org
9am-dusk Mon-Sun

This park is unusually open solely to children and young people – adults can only enter if accompanied by someone under sixteen. There's a small animal enclosure, various playgrounds designed for different age groups and a youth centre which organises a roster of events.

2 THE PEOPLE'S SUPERMARKET

72-78 Lamb's Conduit St, WC1N 3LP
☎ 7430 1827
⌨ www.thepeoplessupermarket.org
8am-10pm Mon-Sat; 10am-9pm Sun

Run 'for the people, by the people', this supermarket is a cooperative venture which asks members to donate £25 a year and four hours of work a month in return for 20 percent off their groceries. As well as stocking produce by local farmers and supporting the local community through jobs, the store runs the People's Kitchen – a hot food station serving cooked lunches at low prices.

3 PERSEPHONE

59 Lamb's Conduit St, WC1N 3NB
☎ 7242 9292
⌨ www.persephonebooks.co.uk
10am-6pm Mon-Fri; noon-5pm Sat

A publisher and bookshop with real purpose, Persephone celebrates literature and non-fiction by neglected and lesser-known twentieth-century female writers. Each volume is beautifully printed in the same way: with a dove-grey book jacket and pretty fabric endpapers.

4 THE FRENCH HOUSE

50 Lamb's Conduit St, WC1N 3LH
☎ 7831 1111 ⌨ www.thefrenchhouse.net
11am-6pm Mon-Sat

Achieve effortless French country style by calling in to this petite boutique which sells Continental textiles, toiletries and homeware sourced from small and artisan manufacturers. The shop layout adds to the rustic feel, with antique dressers and a backroom decked out like a farmhouse kitchen.

5 BEN PENTREATH

17 Rugby St, WC1N 3QT
☎ 7430 2526 ⌨ www.benpentreath.com
11am-6pm Mon-Sat

Interior designer Ben Pentreath and his creative staff have a knack for filling this diminutive shop with covetable and unusual kitchenware, stationery, cushions, prints and more. An ideal place for picking up unique presents.

EXMOUTH MARKET

Exmouth Market – so named during its turn-of-the-twentieth-century role as a bustling market street – suffered crippling decline in the 1970s. Despite efforts to revive its fortunes, it didn't begin to recover its community character until the late 1990s. Chefs Sam and Sam Clark arguably fuelled the change when they opened the acclaimed southern Mediterranean restaurant Moro in 1997, triggering the arrival of a clutch of equally good eateries. Amble up the short, pedestrianised lane on a week day and you'll spy smart restaurants such as Caravan (a modish joint dishing up internationally inspired small plates) and mobile, global food vendors feeding the lunchtime crowds. A medley of gift shops, bookstores and services such as the renowned Family Business Tattoo Shop offer further reasons to visit. At the top of the road, Spa Fields furnishes the area with green space and a grim but fascinating story. In the 1780s, the park was known as the Bone House & Graveyard – a site designated to accommodate 3,000 burials. To the horror of local residents, graveyard manager Mr Bird managed to make room for some 80,000 interments by nightly exhuming and burning bodies. Happily, the landscaped gardens are now an attractive place to catch some rays.

① 3 CORNERS ADVENTURE PLAYGROUND

Northampton Rd, EC1R 0HU
☎ *7527 2975* 🖥 *www.3corners.org.uk*
3.30pm-6pm Tue-Fri; 11am-4.30pm Sat
(times vary during school holidays)

One of the most ambitious and creative park projects in London, 3 Corners Adventure Playground has given children aged six to thirteen a fantastical place to play. Adults are invited to drop off their kids and leave them to enjoy the fully supervised (and free) network of bridges, tunnels, spiral slides, climbing walls and fireman poles.

② CLARKS

46 Exmouth Market, EC1R 4QE
☎ *7837 1974*
10.30am-4pm Mon-Thur;
10.30am-4.30pm Fri-Sat

Clarks has barely changed its fare since it began serving diners in 1960. Meals still consist of meat-filled pastry pies, perfect scoops of mash and lashings of parsley gravy – the wooden café booths and metro tiles are also original.

3 MEDCALF

40 Exmouth Market, EC1R 4QE
☎ 7833 3533 ▯ www.medcalfbar.co.uk
Noon-3pm & 6pm-11pm Mon-Thur;
noon-3pm & 6pm-midnight Fri;
noon-3pm & 6pm-11pm Sat; noon-4pm Sun
There's little sign of the original butcher's shop
Albert Medcalf ran at this address from 1912, but
his spirit lives on in this relaxed British restaurant
which took over the premises in 2003.

4 GN FURNITURE

31 Exmouth Market, EC1R 4QL
☎ 7833 0370 ▯ www.gnfurniture.co.uk
Noon-6pm Mon-Sat; noon-4pm Sun

Discerningly sourced and immaculately restored
mid-twentieth-century furniture is arranged over
two floors in this stylish vintage shop. Pieces
range from the 1950s to the 1980s and include
original textiles, ceramics and glassware.

5 EAST CENTRAL CYCLES

18 Exmouth Market, EC1R 4QE
☎ 7837 0651 ▯ www.eastcentralcycles.co.uk
8am-7pm Mon-Wed; 8am-8pm Thur-Fri;
9am-6pm Sat; 11am-4pm Sun
Whether you're after an off-the-peg bicycle with
a basket or a custom-made road racer, the helpful
bike crew at East Central Cycles are happy to oblige.
The store's bike specialists also tackle repair jobs.

LONDON BRIDGE

FTM

WHITE'S GROUNDS

LEATHERMARKET STREET

BERMONDSEY STREET

TANNER STREET

Bermondsey Street

MOROCCO STREET

TOWER BRIDGE ROAD

LONG LANE

BERMONDSEY SQUARE

5

4

3

2

1

BERMONDSEY STREET

Despite its proximity to Borough Market and the visitor attractions of London Bridge, Bermondsey Street has remained fiercely independent and defiantly local. The peaceful, partly cobbled road rarely shows any sign of tourist overspill, though the presence of iconic contemporary art gallery White Cube goes some way toward encouraging newcomers to the area. Once there, visitors are thrilled with their find: Bermondsey Street proffers an assortment of gift shops and a miscellany of pubs and restaurants. Good gastropubs include The Garrison and The Woolpack, while stellar Spanish chef José Pizarro has two outposts here: tapas bar José and the more roomy restaurant Pizarro. It's these establishments (rather than any central green) that give the long street its current village-like character, though its narrow-fronted shops are hardly new. Bermondsey Street began life as a medieval path for pilgrims travelling to the now long-gone Bermondsey Abbey, and its status as a major thoroughfare was fortified in the nineteenth century when tanneries and workers moved in to support a booming local leather industry.

❶ BERMONDSEY SQUARE ANTIQUES MARKET

Bermondsey Square, SE1 3FD
www.bermondseysquare.co.uk
4am-2pm Fri

Established in 1950, this local market continues to attract serious antiques traders dealing in china, silverware and glass, alongside stallholders hawking more general secondhand clothes and jewellery. A popular farmers' market fills the square on Saturdays (10am-2pm).

❷ SHORTWAVE CINEMA

10 Bermondsey Square, SE1 3UN
☎ *7357 6845* *www.shortwavefilms.com*

Championing the best independent and arthouse movies, Shortwave Cinema schedules a rolling programme of intriguing international film and hosts niche foreign film festivals in support of emerging talent. Its in-house café-bar is perennially packed, though its alfresco, south-facing seating makes it especially attractive come summer.

③ CAVE

210 Bermondsey St, SE1 3TQ
☎ *0011 4701* ⌨ *www.cavelondon.com*
10am-7.30pm Mon-Wed;
10am-8pm Thur-Sat; 11am-6pm Sun

Cave takes care of pre-dinner-party present buying beautifully by rolling a florist, wine cellar and chocolate shop into one. Friendly staff can create a bouquet of fresh-cut blooms, help you navigate the range of bio-dynamic and organic wines, and guide you through the selection of artisan sweets.

④ FASHION AND TEXTILE MUSEUM

83 Bermondsey St, SE1 3XF
☎ *7407 8664* ⌨ *www.ftmlondon.org*
11am-6pm Tue-Sat

It's impossible to miss this striking electric orange and pink museum. Founded by colour- and print-loving designer Zandra Rhodes in 2003, it curates temporary exhibitions, encompasses a café and shop, and runs industry-relevant courses with Newham College.

⑤ LONDON GLASSBLOWING

62-66 Bermondsey St, SE1 3UD
☎ *7403 2800*
🖳 *www.london glassblowing.co.uk*
10am-6pm Mon-Sat

Peter Layton opened this space in 1976, creating a shop-gallery at the front and installing a hot-glass studio out back where you can pull up a chair and watch glassblowers at work. Layton's own glassware is on display in the showroom, along with functional and decorative pieces by other contemporary makers.

VICTORIA

ECCLESTON STREET

EATON SQUARE

ELIZABETH STREET

EBURY STREET

BUCKINGHAM PALACE ROAD

1
2
3
4
5

SLOANE SQUARE

LOWER SLOANE STREET

PIMLICO ROAD

Lower Belgravia

LOWER BELGRAVIA

The genteel Ebury Street runs from Victoria station in the north right down to Pimlico Road in the south – crossing it almost directly in the centre is Elizabeth Street. Here, a small cluster of classy boutiques and their coloured awnings give the sleepy area a jolt of life. The shops are subtly geared toward the wealthy and you'll spy well-to-do women hiding behind their sunglasses as they nip into luxury fragrance store Floris (147 Ebury Street) and dapper gents plumping for a fine bottle of Bordeaux in wine merchants Jeroboams (50 Elizabeth Street). For all the pomp, however, there's a real community spirit in this hidden neighbourhood and the local pubs and cafés are filled with friendly residents.

To get the most out of a visit, arrive via Sloane Square, then head down Lower Sloane Street and take time to explore the dozens of antique and interiors shops along Pimlico Road. En route, make a stop at Orange Square where a bronze statue commemorating the brief residence of Mozart is erected, and a Saturday farmers' market caters for locals. From here, Elizabeth Street is just a couple of minutes' walk.

1 THE THOMAS CUBITT
44 Elizabeth St, SW1W 9PA ☎ *7730 6060*
🖥 *www.thethomascubitt.co.uk*
Noon-11pm Mon-Sat; noon-10.30pm Sun
This smart gastropub channels the spirit of
nineteenth-century master builder Thomas
Cubitt's grand stucco terraces with a regal
country house-style interior. There's a bright and
buzzing bar which spills out on to the street and
formal dining rooms upstairs.

2 MUNGO & MAUD
79 Elizabeth St, SW1W 9PJ ☎ *7022 1207*
🖥 *www.mungoandmaud.com*
10am-6pm Mon-Sat

Rather than garish squeaky toys and synthetic
essentials, pet shop Mungo & Maud finds
harmony between function and aesthetic with
luxury cotton dog beds, wooden bowls, knitted
playthings and hand-stitched leather collars.

3 PHILIP TREACY
69 Elizabeth St, SW1W 9PJ ☎ *7730 3992*
🖥 *www.philiptreacy.co.uk*
10am-6pm Mon-Fri; 11am-5pm Sat
Milliner Philip Treacy started his career on
Elizabeth Street, setting up a studio in the
late fashion icon Isabella Blow's house in 1990.
A few doors down, he continues to showcase
his incredible hats.

④ TOMTOM CIGARS
63 Elizabeth St, SW1W 9PP
☎ *7730 1790* 🖥 *www.tomtom.co.uk*
10am-6pm Mon-Wed; 10am-8pm
Thur-Fri; 11am-6pm Sat; noon-4pm Sun
Indulge a taste for tobacco in this
specialist Cuban cigar store, where you
can sample cigars onsite before you buy.
The shop also sells humidors, accessories
and aged, limited-edition sticks, and has a
sister coffeehouse further down the street.

⑤ PEGGY PORSCHEN
116 Ebury Street, SW1W 9QQ
☎ *7730 1316*
🖥 *www.peggyporschen.com*
10am-6pm Mon-Wed;
10am-7pm Thur-Sat; 10am-6pm Sun
Pretty as a picture, Peggy Porschen's pink
parlour serves fancy cupcakes, biscuits
and cakes. Brides-to-be can discuss their
showstopping tiered creation in the private
boudoir and take inspiration from the
stunning sugarcraft that decorates the
shop's windows.

Du Maire
HOYO DE MONTERREY
3 7/8 x 30

£7.00
£170.00

NORTH

CHALK FARM

Primrose Hill

5

GLOUCESTER AVENUE

2

3

CHALCOT ROAD

FITZROY ROAD

PRINCESS ROAD

SYLVIA
PLATH
1932-1962
POET
lived here
1960-1961

PRIMROSE HILL ROAD

1

REGENT'S PARK ROAD

PRIMROSE
HILL

LONDON
ZOO

PRIMROSE HILL

Primrose Hill residents are fierce in their support for the independent businesses along Regent's Park Road. They've fought off the arrival of a Starbucks in the past and think nothing of rallying together to protect the character of their little community. It helps that the area is often defined by its celebrities, and big names such as Jude Law, Tim Burton and Gwen Stefani have numbered among the locals. This glamorous set followed on the heels of an altogether more bohemian crowd, as the village's now multimillion pound houses have also played home to writers including Sylvia Plath, Alan Bennett and Ian McEwan. It's easy to see the attraction: Regent's Park runs along the south of the village giving easy access to manicured lawns and London Zoo, while the more chaotic delights of Camden are just to the east. Camden's grungy indie scene has had surprisingly little impact on the more demure Primrose Hill. Though when Alan McGee's iconic label Creation Records moved in during the mid-1990s, it gave the peaceful area a new, electric sort of reputation fuelled by the arrival of bands including Oasis – once regulars at neighbourhood pub The Pembroke Castle.

1 PRIMROSE HILL
Primrose Hill Rd, NW3 3NA
🖳 www.royalparks.org.uk
24 hours a day Mon-Sun
William Blake, HG Wells and Blur are among countless writers and bands to have namechecked this 250-foot hill. Kids drag their sledges up here during snowy winters, picnic blankets dot the royal park in summer, and people perennially make their way to the summit for panoramic views of the city.

2 SHEPHERD FOODS
59-61 Regent's Park Rd, NW1 8XD
☎ 7586 4592 🖳 www.shepherdfoods.co.uk
8am-11pm Mon-Sun
A real local asset, this large delicatessen is geared towards those with a refined palate, and its sister deli, Partridges, holds a Royal Warrant for its dedication to supplying the Queen's larder. Shepherd has a decent wine selection and hot food counter making it a great stop before a picnic in the park.

③ PRIMROSE HILL BOOKS
134 Regent's Park Rd, NW1 8XL
☎ *7586 2022* ▯ *www.primrosehillbooks.com*
9.30am–6pm Mon–Fri; 10am–6pm Sat;
11am–6pm Sun

Feeding the minds of Primrose Hill's literary types, this family-run bookshop is on friendly terms with local authors from Alan Bennett to India Knight, and signed books can often be found here. Owners Jessica Graham and Marek Laskowski also organise talks and readings.

④ PRIMROSE BAKERY
69 Gloucester Avenue, NW1 8LD ☎ *7483 4222*
▯ *www.primrosebakery.org.uk*
8.30am–6pm Mon–Sat; 9.30am–5.30pm Sun

Slightly removed from the Hill's main retail hub, the joyously retro Primrose Bakery is worth a detour. Co-founders Martha Swift and Lisa Thomas have created a darling little café serving impeccable cupcakes, cola floats and cookies.

⑤ ROUNDHOUSE
Chalk Farm Rd, NW1 8EH ☎ *7424 9991*
▯ *www.roundhouse.org.uk*

The cylindrical Roundhouse was originally built as a train turntable shed in the 1840s before becoming an arts centre in the 1960s. It's undergone various reincarnations and refurbishments since, but has famously seen Jimi Hendrix, Pink Floyd and the Ramones take to the stage. Today, it programmes a mix of theatre, music and performance art.

ALEXANDRA PALACE

QUEEN'S WOOD

PARK ROAD

MIDDLE LANE

TOTTENHAM LANE

PUB AND DINING
THE QUEENS

Crouch End

CROUCH END HILL

CROUCH HILL

CROUCH HILL

PARKLAND WALK

FINSBURY PARK

1

2

3

4

5

CROUCH END

Although Crouch End can feel a little removed from the city centre,
with no tube and limited bus and rail links, its remoteness is largely its
attraction. Young families love to set up home in this hilly neighbourhood,
essentially hoping to live a suburban lifestyle without actually having to leave
London. And the plan works quite well. Crouch End is a very complete village,
with amenities catering for every need, be it bistro dining, or bedding soil
from the high street garden centre. Its popularity with parents means the roads
surrounding its central clocktower also have a remarkably high concentration of
children's boutiques and mummy-filled cafés – though there's far more to the
area than just shopping and eating. Dominated by farm- and hamlet-studded
woodland until the late nineteenth century, Crouch End still boasts patches
of forest (such as Queen's Wood a mile to the west), while the dominance of
Victorian architecture reflects its era of boom and growth.
The most noteworthy period building is the mighty Alexandra Palace:
some 300 feet above sea-level and surrounded by 196 acres of parkland,
it's a must-visit if you're heading this far north.

① ALEXANDRA PALACE

Alexandra Palace Way, N22 7AY ☎ *8365 2121*
💻 *www.alexandrapalace.com*

Things didn't start well for Ally Pally: the 'People's Palace' was opened to much fanfare in 1873, but promptly burnt down just sixteen days later. It was rebuilt within two years and went on to become a transmitting centre for the BBC from the 1930s to the 1950s. Day-trippers come for peerless views over London, or to visit its cafés, ice-rink, deer enclosure, pitch-and-putt course and glorious boating lake.

② SCARLET RAGE

11 Topsfield Parade, N8 8PR
💻 *www.scarletragevintage.com*
10.30am-6pm Mon-Fri; 11am-6pm Sat; noon-6pm Sun

Vintage dresses from the 1920s to the 1950s hang in immaculate condition in this lovingly arranged boutique. Stylist and owner Jade Stavri is usually on hand with advice on the fit and heritage of the frocks, as well as the array of affordable tea dresses and accessories. Shop dog Frank can be found lounging in the corner.

③ THE HABERDASHERY

22 Middle Lane, N8 8PL ☎ *8342 8098*
💻 *www.the-haberdashery.com*
8am-6pm Mon-Fri; 9am-6pm Sat-Sun

Crouch End is blessed with an abundance of good cafés, but none seem as committed to the community as The Haberdashery. It organises the monthly Barboot (an evening bazaar supporting local artists and makers), as well as exhibitions and gig nights. Peruse its notice board for more village happenings – and try its fluffy bread baked in vintage terracotta pots.

④ THE QUEENS

26 Broadway Parade, N8 9DE
☎ *8340 2031*
💻 *www.thequeenscrouchend.co.uk*
Noon-11pm Mon-Thur; noon-midnight Fri-Sat; noon-11pm Sun

As grand a pub as you'll find in London, The Queens was built as a Victorian hotel and watering hole for Crouch End's refined middle class. Its spectacular stained glass, decorated plaster ceilings and original screened alcoves are lavish, but this is now a very down-to-earth pub.

⑤ PARKLAND WALK

Walk begins at Oxford Rd, N4 3EY
💻 *www.parkland-walk.org.uk*
Dawn-dusk Mon-Sun

This fantastically atmospheric three-mile walk runs from Finsbury Park to Alexandra Palace via a disused train line and is an ideal route if you're planning to explore the area. Follow the wooded path as it rears up over the chimney pots and dips down past abandoned platforms.

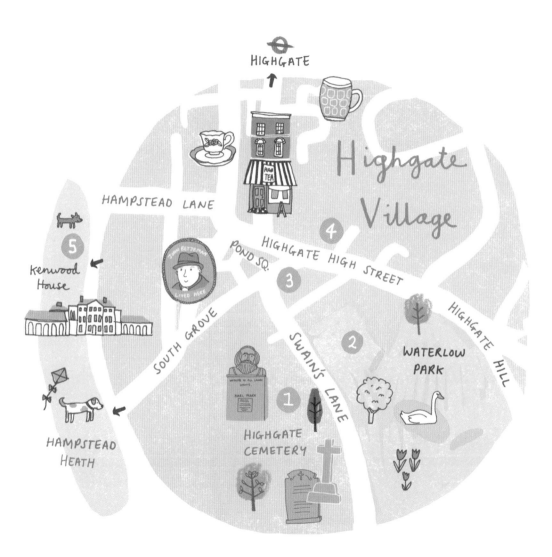

HIGHGATE

Highgate Village

HAMPSTEAD LANE

HIGHGATE HIGH STREET

POND SQ.

SOUTH GROVE

SWAIN'S LANE

HIGHGATE HILL

5
Kenwood House

HAMPSTEAD HEATH

4

3

2
WATERLOW PARK

1
HIGHGATE CEMETERY

JOHN BETJEMAN LIVED HERE

HIGHGATE VILLAGE

Bordering the eastern side of Hampstead Heath and sheltered by woodland, Highgate has long been popular with countryside-craving urbanites looking for a haven within the city. The village's hilltop setting and elevated vantage points have helped give its streets an exclusive air, and the tree-lined lanes and their period mansions have famously played home to poets including Samuel Taylor Coleridge and John Betjeman, as well as musicians George Michael and Ray Davies. But for all its seclusion, historic charm and wealth, this quintessential London village hasn't managed to avoid an influx of chains, and a few faceless coffee shops, supermarkets and pizza restaurants punctuate the high street.

Thankfully, they're neatly hidden behind pretty Georgian shopfronts and caught between more appealing local stores and authentic village pubs. One of the best, The Flask, is a distinctive eighteenth-century drinking den which neighbours quaintly with the picturesque Pond Square (a plaza which hosts community fairs and carol singing) and St Michael's – a grand neo-Gothic church which stands higher than any in London.

① HIGHGATE CEMETERY

Swain's Lane, N6 6PJ ☎ *8340 1834*
🖥 *www.highgate-cemetery.org*
East: 10am-5pm Mon-Fri; 11am-5pm
Sat-Sun. West: by tour only at 1.45pm
Mon-Fri; hourly from 11am to 4pm Sat-Sun
This working, Grade I-listed cemetery split
into two parts is one of the most dramatic
locations in London. Overgrown tombs,
moss-covered statues and extraordinary
vault formations (look out for the Circle of
Lebanon) have made it a site of Victorian
Gothic pilgrimage. Stick to the east for the
graves of Karl Marx and Douglas Adams, or
join a tour to explore the west side's rugged
terrain where Michael Faraday and the family
of Charles Dickens are interred.

② WATERLOW PARK

Highgate Hill, N6 5HF
🖥 *www.waterlowpark.org.uk*
Dawn-dusk Mon-Sun
Once a private estate, this 29-acre plot
was donated to the public by Sir Sydney
Waterlow in 1889 as a 'garden for the
gardenless'. Its undulating lawns, formal
bedding, spring-water ponds and noteworthy
trees are a match for any royal park. The
on-site sixteenth-century Lauderdale House
(which operates as an arts centre) adds
further historic gravitas.

③ HIGHGATE LITERARY & SCIENTIFIC INSTITUTION

11 South Grove, N6 6BS
☎ *8340 3343* 🖥 *www.hlsi.net*
10am-5pm Tue-Fri; 10am-4pm Sat
Established in 1839, this unusual institution
continues to keep locals on their cultural
and intellectual toes with a programme of
challenging film, art, lectures and music.
Its library packs in some 26,000 books and an
archive of Highgate history.

④ HIGH TEA OF HIGHGATE

50 Highgate High St, N6 5HX
☎ *8348 3162*
🖥 *www.highteaofhighgate.com*
10am-6pm Tue-Thur; 8.30am-6pm Fri;
11am-6pm Sat-Sun
There's always a warm welcome at this Highgate
café and owner Georgina Worthington has done
a sterling job of creating a traditional British tea
room with a contemporary twist. Expect classic
cakes served on chintzy crockery.

⑤ KENWOOD HOUSE
Hampstead Lane, NW3 7JR
☎ *8348 1286*
💻 *www.english-heritage.org.uk*

This English Heritage-run Georgian mansion is perched on a knoll on Hampstead Heath looking out over a tranquil lake. Basking bodies speckle its lawns come summer, though the real treasures are inside where an art collection features work by Rembrandt, Gainsborough, Vermeer and Turner.

CAMDEN PASSAGE

Though not a defined village in the traditional sense, Camden Passage is distinct enough to provide a picturesque antidote to Islington's homogenous Upper Street which runs parallel. The mid-eighteenth-century lane became a hub for antiques in the 1960s, and though the number of traders has declined in recent years, some 150 dealers still display their wares come Wednesday and Saturday market days. There's also a strong vintage and antiques focus to the permanent independent businesses that line the alleyway. Try Annie's at number 12 for an opulent and girly mix of mink pelts, 1920s dresses and antique lace; or pop into Odyssey at number 47 for twentieth-century glass, furniture and lighting.

The compact passage also has a number of excellent eateries, and droves of people flock here at the weekends hoping to bag a table for brunch at The Breakfast Club, eat lunch at gastropub The Elk in the Woods, or buy a cone of Italian ice cream from Zucono. If you'd rather avoid the hustle, it's best to visit mid-week when Camden Passage's clamour mellows and the shopping streets around the little road also become more pleasant to explore.

1 FELIX & LILY'S
3 Camden Passage, N1 8EA
☎ 7424 5423 💻 www.felixandlilys.com
10am-6pm Mon-Fri; 10am-7pm Sat;
11am-5pm Sun

Be warned: tots with a penchant for fashion
may well turn into demanding little terrors in
this children's boutique. Princess tutus, nostalgic
printed tees, trendy shirts and classic blazers
hang cutely from the rails, and classic toys
(a wooden doll's house, for example) fill
the shelves.

2 SMUG
13 Camden Passage, N1 8EA
☎ 7354 0253 💻 www.ifeelsmug.com
11am-6pm Wed; noon-7pm Thur;
11am-6pm Fri-Sat; noon-5pm Sun

Local interior and graphic designer Lizzie Evans
spent her pocket money in Camden Passage as
a teenager and was thrilled when this three-
floor store became available in 2007. Her eye
for design is evident in the covetable mix of
handmade toys, printed textiles and retro
kitchenware and stationery.

③ PIERREPONT ARCADE

*Pierrepont Row (off Camden Passage),
N1 8EG* ☎ *7359 0190*
🖥 *www.camdenpassageislington.co.uk*
Shop: times vary
Market: 8am-4pm Wed & Sat

A cluster of cupboard-sized shops make up this quaint antiques arcade, with further dealers manning stalls at its entrance on market days. Each is dedicated to a specific product, making this is an ideal place to get expert advice on buying antique clocks, oriental porcelain, period jewellery, military memorabilia and more.

④ KIPFERL

20 Camden Passage, N1 8ED
☎ *7704 1555* 🖥 *www.kipferl.co.uk*
9am-10pm Tue-Sat; 10am-10pm Sun

Somewhat under-represented in London, Austrian food has found a champion in Kipferl. The café and restaurant has a sleek aesthetic and turns out classic sachertorte and apfelstrudel together with smooth Viennese coffee served the traditional way: on a metal tray with a glass of water. For lunch and dinner, try a belly-warming beef goulash or Wiener schnitzel.

⑤ LOOP

15 Camden Passage, N1 8EA
☎ 7288 1160 🖥 www.loopknitting.com
11am-6pm Tue-Wed; 11am-7.30pm Thur;
11am-6pm Fri-Sat; noon-5pm Sun

More than just a yarn shop, Loop fosters a craft community. Its monthly SOS drop-ins help knitters in a bind and its knitting and crochet classes cater for beginners and improvers. The shop itself brings together a medley of colourful yarns, interesting patterns and beautiful gifts made by skilled knit, crochet and felt designers.

STOKE NEWINGTON CHURCH STREET

You'd be hard pushed to find a London village with a more
proactive community than Stoke Newington. Locals are quick to
club together to launch campaigns against big businesses trying to move into
the indie-spirited Church Street, and support myriad events from
craft fairs in Abney Public Hall to the all-organic Saturday farmers' market
at St Paul's Church. Keeping it local – and keeping it green –
is a primary concern for Stoke Newington's residents, and not-for-profit
initiatives (such as the organic veg-box scheme Growing Communities)
tend to flourish. This type of social enterprise makes Stokey an
attractive option for young families, and you might well be shunted
off the pavement by pram congestion if you arrive on a busy weekend.
Luckily, there are copious places to dive into until the rush has died down.
Pubs The Three Crowns and The Jolly Butchers are at the heart
of the village, as are laid-back Italian restaurant Homa and breakfast-favourite
The Blue Legume. Come evening, evidence of an overspill from
nearby nightlife hub Dalston becomes obvious, as a handful of clubs
and bars keep revellers entertained.

① CLISSOLD PARK

Stoke Newington Church St, N16 9HJ
☎ 8356 8428 ▣ www.hackney.gov.uk/parks
Dawn-dusk Mon-Sun

Clissold isn't just a space for lounging and picnicking: it's an activities park. The playground and paddling pool become packed with children on a balmy day when families also turn up for the animal enclosure, butterfly dome and aviary. A sports pitch, tennis courts and good café in the stately Clissold House complete the park package.

② STOKE NEWINGTON TOWN HALL

Stoke Newington Church St, N16 0JR
☎ 8356 5505 ▣ www.hackney.gov.uk

Regular retro dance evenings at this Art Deco town hall bring back a touch of the building's mid-twentieth-century glamour, when the cool kids would spend their nights tearing up the dancefloor in the Assembly Hall. The venue also continues the tradition of hosting comedy and concerts, and has added a film club to its entertainment programme.

③ THE SPENCE BAKERY & CAFÉ

161 & 178 Stoke Newington Church St, N16 0UH
☎ 7254 9753 ▣ www.thespence.co.uk
Bakery: 8am-6pm Mon-Sat; 9am-6pm Sun
Café: 9am-6pm Mon-Sun

The Spence's moreish, daily-baked bread can be enjoyed both in the original bakery (161), and its second, larger café (178). You'll have to be patient, however, as both establishments can get incredibly busy with punters queuing for seasonal loaves, lovely cakes and cups of coffee.

④ JOHN'S GARDEN CENTRE

175 Stoke Newington Church St, N16 0UL
☎ 7275 9494
▣ www.johns-gardencentre.co.uk
8.30am-6pm Mon-Sat; 10am-5pm Sun

Supplying green-fingered residents with all they need to keep their gardens growing, John's knows its local market well and stocks a solid range of organic compost, veg plants, herbs and pesticides. The pot plants, trees, tools and terracotta are all out back.

⑤ NOOK

153 Stoke Newington Church St, N16 0UH
☎ 7249 9436 ▣ www.nookshop.co.uk
11am-6pm Mon-Sat; 11am-5pm Sun

You'll find several Stokey stores selling interesting homeware, but this sleek boutique is particularly worth noting. The emphasis is on beautifully designed products, be it an ever-useful dustpan and brush, or colourful cushions by Donna Wilson. Small, Scandi-style furniture, screenprints by local artists and handmade ceramics also feature.

Fenton House

JOHN
CONSTABLE
1776 - 1837
Painter
lived
here

HAMPSTEAD
HEATH

HEATH STREET

HOLLY HILL

5

⊖ HAMPSTEAD

FLASK WALK

GAYTON ROAD

WILLOW ROAD

PILGRIM'S LANE

KEATS GROVE

1

2 3

HAMPSTEAD HIGH STREET

Hampstead
Village

HAMPSTEAD VILLAGE

One of London's most iconic villages, lofty Hampstead looks like it's been sliced straight out of the countryside. Narrow, winding lanes and Victorian cottages provide bucolic character, while its more than fair share of historic attractions ensure Hampstead is never forgotten as a key London destination. Two National Trust properties provide some of the area's most prized gems: Fenton House – a seventeenth-century merchant's townhouse famed for its period furnishings and enchanting walled garden – and 2 Willow Road, a modernist villa which reveals more about Hampstead's artsy and intellectual 1930s heyday. This property (originally home to architect Ernö Goldfinger, a name famously borrowed by disgruntled neighbour and Bond author Ian Fleming) is particularly recommended, brimming as it is with art and furniture by luminaries including Henry Moore and Max Ernst. It's also just tripping distance from Keats House, and the former homes of John Constable, DH Lawrence and Stanley Spencer are also nearby. In fact, the network of roads either side of Hampstead's now largely chain-filled high street are teeming with literary and artistic heritage, and it's worth arriving armed with a Blue Plaque guide.

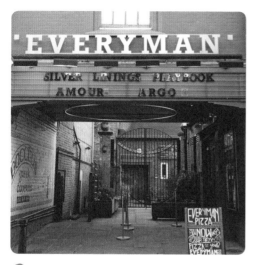

① EVERYMAN CINEMA

5 Holly Bush Vale, NW3 6TX
☎ *0871 906 9060*
🖳 *www.everymancinema.com*

Opened in 1933, this outpost of the boutique Everyman cinema chain is one of the oldest movie theatres in the UK. It's also one of the most sophisticated, with two-person sofas, an alcohol licence and waiter service.

② HAMPSTEAD ANTIQUE AND CRAFT EMPORIUM

12 Heath St, NW3 6TE ☎ *7794 3297*
🖳 *www.hampsteadantiqueemporium.com*
10.30am-5.30pm Tue-Fri; 10am-6pm Sat; 10.30am-5.30pm Sun

More than twenty specialist dealers man their own cubby-like spaces in this ramshackle and old-fashioned indoor emporium which opened in 1967. The early noughties saw craftmakers join the antique sellers, and you'll now find handmade jewellery and ceramics alongside vintage furniture, textiles and collectable toys.

③ HAMPSTEAD COMMUNITY CENTRE

78 Hampstead High St, NW3 1RE
☎ 7794 8313
Vendors: 9am-5pm Mon-Sat
Food market: 10am-5pm Sat

A grocer, butcher and fishmonger do brisk week-round business outside this centre, joined by food traders indoors selling fresh produce and hot food on Saturdays. On Sundays, a rotating market alternately covers antiques, bric-à-brac, books and crafts.

④ THE FLASK

14 Flask Walk, NW3 1HG   ☎ 7435 4580
▨ www.theflaskhampstead.co.uk
11am-11pm Mon-Thur; 11am-midnight Fri-Sat; noon-10.30pm Sun

Occupying a historic plot where fresh water was bottled and sold in the early eighteenth century, the Grade II-listed Flask was built on the site of the Thatched House pub in 1874. As well as commemorating the location's heritage, the pub offers up its own antiquities, with original glass screens, and panels painted by Belgian artist Jan Van Beers.

**⑤ BURGH HOUSE
& HAMPSTEAD MUSEUM**
New End Square, NW3 1LT
☎ *7431 0144* 🖥 *www.burghhouse.org.uk*
*Noon-5pm Wed-Sun (Sat ground-floor
gallery and café only)*
This Grade I-listed house was built as a residence
in 1704, turned into a British militia HQ in
the mid-nineteenth century and was home to
Rudyard Kipling's daughter in the 1930s before
becoming a community hub some twenty years
later. In 1979, it was restored and transformed
into a museum and arts centre which celebrates
the colourful history of Hampstead Village.

SOUTH

EAST DULWICH

BRIXTON

BROCKWELL PARK

East Dulwich

GROVE VALE

EAST DULWICH GROVE

LORDSHIP LANE

BLUE BRICK CAFE
CAFE

NORTH CROSS ROAD

FELLBRIGG ROAD

Dulwich Park and Picture Gallery

DULWICH VILLAGE

LORDSHIP LANE

BARRY ROAD

Horniman museum

1

2 4

3

5

EAST DULWICH

Part of a vast, leafy south London suburb bookended by Brixton and Peckham, East Dulwich is one of several local villages and attractions. Annoyingly, the distances between each can be prohibitive if you're walking, so it's best to make a transport plan if you want to head down for the day and take in the Art Deco lido at Brockwell Park, the anthropological Horniman Museum and Gardens, and the bucolic Dulwich Village and Dulwich Picture Gallery – a majestic Regency building housing an impressive collection of Old Masters. Leave plenty of time for East Dulwich, however, as it hosts the area's largest concentration of shops and eateries. The main mishmash of retail can be found along the mile-long high street Lordship Lane, though the far quieter side street North Cross Road is also a hotspot. A sort of village in itself, North Cross is home to the popular Blue Mountain Coffee Shop, confectioners Hope & Greenwood, and vintage emporiums including ChiChiRaRa and North Cross Vintage (on Fellbrigg Road). It also lays on a fashionable Saturday market made up of retro clothes stalls and vendors selling hot and fresh food.

① COLOUR MAKES PEOPLE HAPPY

53 Grove Vale, SE22 8EQ ☎ 7207 1120
🖳 www.sieclecolours.com
10am-6pm Tue-Sat; 11am-4pm Sun

Simon March avoids loading his paint hues with stories about their heritage, or matching them with other shades. Instead, his various emulsions (designed by him and made by Dutch specialists) are painted on to hanging clogs and given throwaway names such as 'I thought I told you to wait in the car'.

② ROULLIER WHITE

125 Lordship Lane, SE22 8HU
☎ 8693 5150
🖳 www.roullierwhite.com
10am-6pm Mon-Sat; 11am-5pm Sun

If you tend to reach for the bicarb and vinegar when a household emergency strikes, you'll love Roullier White's line of traditional and practical household products. Among nostalgically packaged laundry detergent, furniture polish and washing-up liquid, the store stocks grooming essentials, artisan perfumes, luxury gifts and homeware.

③ FRANKLIN'S
157 Lordship Lane, SE22 8HX
☎ *8299 9598* 🖥 *www.franklinsrestaurant.com*
Noon-11pm Mon-Wed; noon-midnight Thur-Fri;
10am-midnight Sat; noon-11pm Sun
There's no shortage of places to eat in East Dulwich, but none have quite the dedication to localism as Franklin's. The restaurant's menu makes use of fresh produce from Kent, meat from rare breed farms and seafood fished from British waters. Next door, Franklin's Farm Shop stocks the raw ingredients.

④ BLUE BRICK CAFÉ
14 Fellbrigg Rd (off North Cross Rd), SE22 9HH
☎ *8299 8670 9am-6pm Mon-Sat; 10am-6pm Sun*
The sleek Luca's Bakery at number 145, and tea salon Le Chandelier at 161, are two of Lordship Lane's best cafés, but this slightly out-of-the-way establishment deserves special mention. Clad in blue tiles on a residential road, the café serves a vegetarian and vegan all-day menu in what looks like grandma's kitchen. Stop in for cake and coffee, or bring your own bottle to pair with stews and salads.

⑤ DULWICH LIBRARY
368 Lordship Lane, SE22 8NB
☎ *7525 2000* 🖥 *www.southwark.gov.uk*
9am-8pm Mon; 10am-8pm Tue; 9am-8pm Wed-Fri;
9am-5pm Sat; noon-4pm Sun
Established in 1897, this grand, redbrick library doubles up as a community hub hosting adult reading groups (from manga to poetry), as well as toddler mornings, after-school clubs, film matinées and craft workshops.

HOLLY GROVE

PECKHAM RYE

CASH & CARRY

Bellenden
Road

BLENHEIM GROVE

BELLENDEN ROAD

CHOUMERT GROVE

RYE LANE

CHADWICK ROAD

review 131

3

2

CHOUMERT ROAD

1

4

5

FLOCK X HERD
BUTCHERY

BELLENDEN ROAD

Parts of Peckham may be a little down-at-heel, but gentrification has had its grip on the south London district for some time, and places such as Bellenden Road are the fashionable result. The serene, boutique-lined street seems at odds with the parallel Rye Lane where pound shops and African grocery stores butt up against the odd pop-up bar – usually frequented by art school students from the nearby Camberwell College. The contrast often sees Bellenden Road accused of being 'posh' rather than 'real' Peckham, though it's impossible to fault its genial shopkeepers, and hard to resist its pleasant cafés (Anderson & Co), proper butchers (Flock & Herd) and welcoming pubs. Independently owned boozer The Montpelier on Choumert Road has a dinky cinema in its backroom and serves local brews, while The Victoria Inn back on Bellenden is at the heart of the village with a dog-friendly policy and children's playroom. The surrounding area definitely merits a ramble too: look out for arts centre The Bussey Building at 133 Rye Lane, Persian deli Persepolis at 28 Peckham High Street, and the café-cum-gallery that pops up on top of the Peckham Rye Multistorey Car Park each summer.

1 CAFÉ VIVA
44 Choumert Rd, SE15 4SE
www.cafeviva.co.uk
7.30am-5pm Tue-Fri; 9am-5pm Sat-Sun
Café Viva's humble interior (bare-brick walls and simple white tables) serves as a fitting backdrop to a modest, well-executed menu of homemade soups, sandwiches and cakes. Locally sourced food is a feature, and coffee comes from close-by roastery Volcano Coffee Works.

2 REVIEW
131 Bellenden Rd, SE15 4QY ☎ 7639 7400
www.reviewbookshop.co.uk
10am-7pm Tue-Sat; 11am-5pm Sun
Local novelist Evie Wyld runs this bookshop and encourages a 'balanced reading diet' by stocking a generous number of short story and poetry collections among novels and non-fiction. The shop is a pivotal part of the annual Peckham Literary Festival and also hosts regular in-store events.

③ FENTON WALSH

117 Bellenden Rd, SE15 4QY
☎ *7635 0033*
🖥 *www.fentonwalsh.com*
10.30am-6pm Mon;
10am-6pm Tue-Thur;
10am-7pm Fri; 10am-6pm Sat;
11am-5pm Sun

This fashion boutique was here well before Bellenden Road made a name for itself, and owner Maria Fenton has long championed the area by rallying support for summer parties, Christmas fairs and shopping events. She also finds time to source an impeccable array of affordable threads and accessories by independent designers.

4 THE BEGGING BOWL
168 Bellenden Rd, SE15 4BW
☎ *7635 2627*
🖥 *www.thebeggingbowl.co.uk*
6pm-10pm Tue-Wed; noon-2.30pm
& 6pm-10pm Thur-Sat

Thai street food is brought indoors by regional food expert and chef Jane Alty in this colourful, contemporary restaurant. The atmosphere is jumping in the evenings, when busy tables are topped with small bowls (stir-fries, soups, grills and curries) designed for sociable sharing.

5 MELANGE CHOCOLATE SHOP & CAFE
184 Bellenden Rd, SE15 4BW
🖥 *www.themelange.com*
Noon-7pm Tue-Fri; 10am-6pm Sat-Sun

Bowls of sample chocolate are lined up along the counter inviting you try inventive flavour combinations such as ginger and lime, cardamom and clove, or raspberry and rosemary. The chocs (or a heavy slice of cake) can be wrapped up to go, or you can learn more about the infused Belgian sweets at Melange's tasting and making workshops.

BRIXTON ≷

Brixton Village

ATLANTIC ROAD

POPES ROAD

BRIXTON

FRESH Coley + FRESH POLLOCK

ELECTRIC AVENUE

2.99

4.20

MARKET ROW

3RD AVE
2ND AVENUE
1
4TH AVE
2
5TH AVE
3
6TH AVE
1ST AVENUE

Circus

HONEST

4
5

BE 70   SPECIMEN

COLDHARBOUR LANE

BRIXTON VILLAGE

The late-noughties revival of Brixton Village and the adjacent Market Row kickstarted a new era for this once depressed south London quarter. At the time, the arched arcades (parts of which were installed as early as the 1930s) were in desperate need of tenants and repair, and a campaign to encourage new business through low rents managed to entice a handful of resourceful locals with bright ideas to set up shop. Within a couple of years, the two covered passageways had become a London hotspot, and now dozens of restaurants, cafés and boutiques jostle alongside the arcades' older Caribbean delis, fresh fish stalls and African textile shops. This unique, multicultural urban village continues to be a much-lauded destination with celebrated restaurants such as Honest Burgers, larder shops including Cornercopia (which only stocks locally sourced foods), and bakeries like Wild Caper. Regular shoppers tend to use the Brixton Pound – a private currency which helps money stay within the village – and the sociable market community is always game for organising parties and late night shopping events, or simply pointing you in the direction of one of the arcades' many entry and exit points.

1 LEFTOVERS

Unit 71, Fourth Avenue, SW9 8PS
www.facebook.com/leftoversbrixton
11am-5.30pm Tue-Wed; 11am-10pm Thur;
11am-5.30pm Fri-Sat; noon-4pm Sun

Margot Waggoner makes regular trips to France to source vintage clothes and accessories for her treasure-trove of a store. Call by to pick up a Parisian petticoat, a Breton top, some antique lace or one of the many Continental trinkets she brings back from her travels.

2 CIRCUS

Unit 70, Fifth Avenue, SW9 8PR
www.circus5thave.blogspot.co.uk
11pm-5pm Tue-Wed; 11am-10pm Thur;
11am-8pm Fri-Sat; 11am-4pm Sun

Tabitha Rout and Binki Taylor, owners of this compact boutique, champion local artists with unrelenting dedication. They keep the Circus shelves stocked with an ever-changing line-up of handmade ceramics, cards, jewellery and art by practitioners who live within a five-mile radius of the store – and they make sure price tags remain affordable.

3 FEDERATION COFFEE

Unit 77-78, Fifth Avenue, SW9 8PS
www.federationcoffee.com
8am-5pm Mon-Fri; 9am-6pm Sat;
9am-5pm Sun

Run by two Kiwis, Federation was one of the originators of Brixton Market's current boom and its popularity has seen it up size to larger premises. Its success rests on its locally roasted coffee and freshly baked cakes and pastries.

4 CANNON & CANNON

18 Market Row, SW9 8LD ☎ 7501 9152
www.cannonandcannon.com
11am-5pm Tue-Wed; 11am-9pm Thur-Fri;
9am-9pm Sat; 11am-5pm Sun

Cannon & Cannon can sort cheese and charcuterie board dilemmas with minimal fuss. Its selection of British cured meat (sourced from as close as Kent and as far as the Scottish Highlands) is matched by a stellar range of artisan cheese. Pair with the deli's chutneys and pickles, and wash down with pale ale from Bermondsey's Kernel Brewery.

5 FRANCO MANCA

4 Market Row, SW9 8LD ☎ 7738 3021
www.francomanca.co.uk
Noon-5pm Mon-Wed; noon-10pm Thur-Fri;
11.30am-10pm Sat; noon-5pm Sun

One of the first restaurants to put Brixton Village on the map, Franco Manca has become so famous for its mouthwatering sourdough pizzas, you can expect a queue to come snaking out of the door most evenings. There are plenty of worthy alternatives should you be short of time.

SOUTH KENSINGTON

ELYSTAN STREET

WHITEHEAD'S GROVE

SLOANE SQUARE

TOM'S KITCHEN

THE CHELSEA FISHMONGER

5

4

CALE STREET

3

2

1

GODFREY STREET

JUBILEE PLACE

SYDNEY STREET

Chelsea Green

CHELSEA GREEN

Tight-lipped residents don't like to reveal too much about this locale, preferring to preserve the peace of their secret village. To their credit, they've done a marvellous job – many Londoners are clueless about Chelsea Green's existence, missing out on an intimate little neighbourhood with a traditional squared-off lawn at its centre. The roads facing the green – and additionally Elystan Street – are where you'll find a small number of boutiques, bars and grocers supplying high-grade essentials. Look out for gourmet food shop The Pie Man, the acclaimed Chelsea Fishmonger, Jago Butchers and wine shop Haynes, Hanson & Clark. If you'd rather stop for food, the village also offers two destination restaurants headed up by the same chef: formal dining room Tom Aikens and the more relaxed British brasserie Tom's Kitchen. It would be a shame to visit solely for a meal, however, as just a short walk away, Sydney Street reveals the magnificent St Luke's & Christ Church. The imposing neo-Gothic nineteenth-century building is quite rightly proud of its heritage: Charles Dickens married Catherine Hogarth here on April 2 1836, just two days after publication of his first instalment of The Pickwick Papers.

❶ FELT

13 Cale St, SW3 3QS ☎ 7349 8829
🖳 www.felt-london.com
10am-6pm Mon-Sat

A cult favourite, and beloved by celebrities, this tiny shop is crammed with an unusual mix of vintage and new costume and fine jewellery. The cherry-picked selection sits alongside an oddball mix of ever-changing gifts from rare books and antique ceramics to colourful cashmere scarves. If you're strapped for cash, you can bring along a piece of jewellery you no longer wear, and barter it for store credit.

❷ CHELSEA TOYS

53 Godfrey St, SW3 3SX ☎ 7352 1718
🖳 www.chelseatoys.co.uk
10am-5.30pm Mon-Thur;
10am-6pm Fri-Sat

It may jar with our digital age, but the old-fashioned Chelsea Toys should thrill even the most technologically savvy child with its seductive assortment of nostalgic wooden toys, Victorian games, cap guns, mobiles, finger puppets, soft animals and crafts.

③ FIFI WILSON

1 Godfrey St, SW3 3TA ☎ *7352 3232*
🖳 *www.fifiwilson.com*
10am-6pm Mon-Sat

Fifi Wilson's reputation for selling labels you're unlikely to see elsewhere has broken beyond Chelsea Green, and it's not uncommon to see a big-name model or actress browsing the rails for girly pieces by lesser-known and international boutique designers.

④ JANE ASHER PARTY CAKES & SUGAR CRAFT
22-24 Cale St, SW3 3QU ☎ *7584 6177*
🖥 *www.janeasher.com*
9.30am-5.30pm Mon-Sat

The sweet smell of icing greets you at the doorway of Jane Asher's baking shop. The one-time fiancée of Paul McCartney set up shop in 1990, selling biscuit cutters, cake colouring, ribbons, decorations, silver boards and more. Friendly staff can advise you on executing a one-off celebration cake, or you can commission a sugarcraft creation from the skilled onsite bakers.

⑤ PAPER & PAINT LIBRARY
3 Elystan St, SW3 3NT ☎ *7823 7755*
🖥 *www.paintlibrary.co.uk*
9am-5pm Mon-Fri; 10am-4pm Sat

Joining a run of interiors specialists on Elystan Street, David Oliver's Paper & Paint Library is devoted to pairing harmonious hues for effortless home-decorating. Each emulsion and wallpaper shade is uniquely created by David, who travels the world looking for colour inspiration.

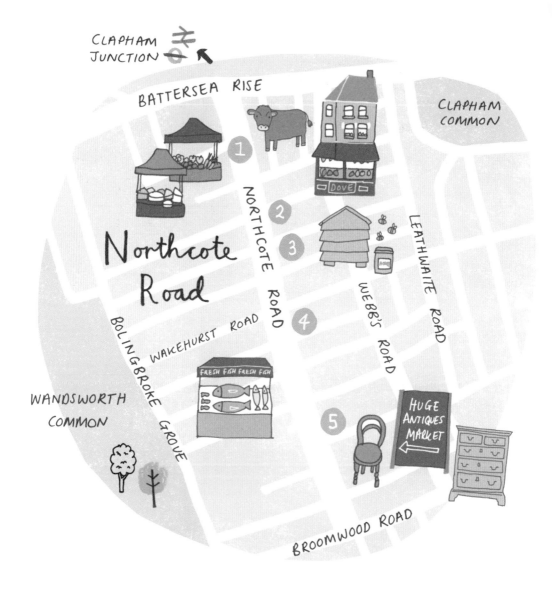

NORTHCOTE ROAD

Once farmland and fields of lavender, this area of Battersea
blossomed following the advent of Victorian railways and industrialisation.
Terraces sprouted around key thoroughfares, and the Falcon Brook
(whose route ran along the path of Northcote Road) was lost from the landscape.
As the population grew, so did small shopping enclaves such as Northcote
Road: it was here that locals would run grocery errands to the butchers, bakers
and fishmongers, as well as the famous fruit and veg market. The road changed
with the times during the twentieth century, but has always retained its
market tradition and continues to foster independent business, both foodie and
otherwise. For the best boutiques and cafés, it pays to head away from
Clapham Junction's uninspiring high street and toward the lower end of
Northcote Road. Make an effort to walk over to the parallel (and far quieter)
Webb's Road too, where there's a small congregation of shops and eateries.
If you're all shopped out, try Battersea Rise to the north for a decent bar,
or head east or west to hit green space: Northcote Road is sandwiched
between Wandsworth Common and Clapham Common.

① NORTHCOTE ROAD MARKET

Northcote Rd, SW11 1PA
☎ *8871 6384*
🖳 *www.wandsworth.gov.uk*
8am-6pm Mon-Sun
This outdoor market really gets going on Fridays and Saturdays when there's a full complement of stalls selling fruit, veg, household goods and bric-à-brac. Some of the best traders are around all week, however, meaning you can pick up superb loaves, pizzas and gigantic doughnuts at Breadstall, or fresh seafood at South Coast Fisheries.

② DOVE

71 Northcote Rd, SW11 6PJ
☎ *7223 5191*
🖳 *www.doveandson.co.uk*
8.30pm-5pm Mon; 8.30pm-5.30pm Tue-Fri; 8.30pm-5pm Sat; 10am-3pm Sun
Three generations of the Dove family have stood behind the counter since this butcher was founded in 1889. Bob Dove is currently at the helm, and can usually be found recommending

a particular handmade sausage or piece of Yorkshire beef, or serving a legendary homemade pie. The shop keeps good gastronomic company with nearby wine merchant Philglas & Swiggot and cheese shop Hamish Johnston.

③ THE HIVE HONEY SHOP
93 Northcote Rd, SW11 6PL
☎ *7924 6233*
🖥 *www.thehivehoneyshop.co.uk*
10am-5pm Mon-Tue; 10am-2pm Wed; 10am-5pm Thur-Sat (closed 1pm-2pm)
Honey-based beauty products, candles, lozenges, condiments, ciders, sweets and more are tightly packed into this small shop opened by James Hamill in 1992. The Hamill family have been apiarists since the 1920s, and this store (which features a live hive) shows off international and local honey, and also arranges urban beekeeping workshops for beginners.

④ VERDE LONDON
113 Northcote Rd (via Wakehurst Rd), SW11 6PJ ☎ *7223 2095*
🖥 *www.verde.co.uk*
10am-5.30pm Mon-Sat
Essential oils and botanicals are key ingredients in this shop's natural and organic products. Its creams, shampoos and bath salts – as well as remedies for specific ailments – all smell divine, and knowledgeable staff are exceptionally helpful.

❺ NORTHCOTE ROAD ANTIQUES MARKET

155A Northcote Rd, SW11 6QB
☎ *7228 6850*
🖵 *www.spectrumsoft.net*
10am-6pm Mon-Sat;
noon-5pm Sun

Some thirty dealers cover a variety of homeware periods and styles in this indoor antique emporium – you'll find casual visitors cooing over retro curiosities, and collectors making investments in silver, china and furniture.

ABBEVILLE VILLAGE

This short Victorian shopping parade on Abbeville Road cemented its community character in the late 1990s when it began to be referred to as Abbeville Village. Since then, local house prices have shot up and the road's amenities have become a muddle of chichi boutiques, bistros and estate agents. A couple of overly familiar high street chains have crept in, but by-and-large the village has maintained its picturesque, period feel – it's also remained a relatively local secret, relying on its detached location (away from Clapham's more obvious shopping districts and main roads) to protect its peaceful personality.

The eastern side of Clapham Common flanks Abbeville Road, and a few stray dog walkers and pram-pushers find themselves sauntering over to this neighbourhood for events and markets organised by sociable residents.

The street comes together for a June fête each summer, and there's a sizeable Christmas fair come winter. The rest of the year sees a weekly Sunday famers' market crop up off Abbeville Road on Bonneville Gardens, and the local church on Narbonne Avenue hosts a book club, Guides and children's ballet classes.

① THE ABBEVILLE

67-69 Abbeville Rd, SW4 9JW
☎ 8675 2201 ⌨ www.theabbeville.co.uk
11am-11pm Mon-Wed; 11am-midnight
Thur-Sat; 11am-10.30pm Sun

Three locals addressed a need for a village
hangout in 2002 with this smart and distinctly
pastoral pub and dining room. The seasonal
menu makes use of animals reared through
the pub's own breeding programmes set up in
conjunction with small British farms. The chefs
also pride themselves on nose-to-tail cooking.

② WHISPERS

51 Abbeville Rd, SW4 9JX ☎ 8675 7700
⌨ www.whispersbeauty.com
11am-5pm Mon; 10am-7pm Tue-Wed;
10am-8pm Thur; 10am-7pm Fri;
10am-6pm Sat; 11am-5pm Sun

This boutique beauty salon feels like a plush living
room, with its opulent chandelier and white sofas.
Friendly therapists add to the relaxed ambience,
and services range from indulgent massages to
essential waxing and manicures.

3 LES SARDINES

63 Abbeville Rd, SW4 9JW
☎ *8675 3900*
🖳 *www.lessardines.co.uk*
10am-5.30pm Tue-Sat;
11am-3pm Sun

There's a certain French *mien* to this interiors store: rustic linens are sold by the metre (or made into deluxe cushions and used to decorate antique armoires) and Duralex glass tumblers beg to be bought and filled with wine. You can pop in to pick up a luxury candle, or arrive with a mind to invest in a handcrafted oak dining table.

④ ABBEVILLE KITCHEN
47 Abbeville Rd, SW4 9JX ☎ *8772 1110*
🖳 *www.abbevillekitchen.com*
Noon-3pm & 6.30pm-10.30pm Tue-Sat;
1pm-3pm & 6pm-9.30pm Sun
A local favourite, this laid-back restaurant
was opened by Kevin Hastings, the man
behind the brilliant Le Petit Boulanger
a few doors down. It features an open
kitchen which turns out a no-fuss menu
of modern European small plates and
main dishes.

⑤ MACFARLANE'S DELI
48 Abbeville Rd, SW4 9NF ☎ *8673 5373*
🖳 *www.macfarlanesdeli.co.uk*
8.30am-7pm Mon-Fri;
8.30am-6pm Sat; 10am-5.30pm Sun
Robert Marsham, formerly co-head of
hospitality at Fortnum & Mason, runs
this deli with knowledge and care. His
first-grade selection of international
cheeses, meats, wine and fine foods are
meticulously sourced, and the deli's
own-made sausage rolls have earned
legendary status.

EAST

Whitecross Village

5 IRONMONGER ROW BATHS

OLD STREET

HULA NAILS

4

3

WHITECROSS STREET

FORTUNE STREET

BUNHILL ROW BURIAL GROUND

2

WILLIAM BLAKE POET
CATHERINE SOPHIA

BUNHILL ROW

CHISWELL STREET

1 BARBICAN CENTRE

SILK STREET

BARBICAN

WHITECROSS VILLAGE

Though technically sporting a central London postcode,
Whitecross Village is just striking distance from Shoreditch in the east,
and best explored together with other villages in this chapter. Try to arrive
at lunch, as its main calling card is the weekday food market which brings
Whitecross Street roaring to life from around midday. City workers, nearby
residents and local shopkeepers descend on the area to ogle the many hot food
carts that pitch up as they queue for fresh burritos, curries, bagels, falafels, pies
and more. If you are heading over for lunch, make a note of Fortune Street Park
at the bottom end of the road, where an abundance of benches provide mealtime
seating. Or else head to the Two Brewers at 121 Whitecross Street – a pub that
invites you to bring your boxed-up takeaway inside to enjoy with a pint.
You can always round off with a visit to Fix at number 161, where baristas use
lip-smacking seasonal coffee blends. Aside from foodie nourishment,
the road also provides an easy thoroughfare between the Barbican Centre
in the south, and chamber music venue London Symphony Orchestra
St Luke's in the north.

THE ROAST OF SH

① BARBICAN CENTRE

Silk St, EC2Y 8DS ☎ 7638 8891
🖥 www.barbican.org.uk
9am-11pm Mon-Sat; noon-11pm Sun

The Brutalist architecture of this mammoth building rears up above Whitecross Village. More than a decade in the making, it was opened in 1982 and remains one of the largest arts centres in Europe, curating a cutting-edge programme of music, theatre, art and film.

② BUNHILL FIELDS BURIAL GROUND

38 City Rd, EC1Y 1AU
🖥 www.cityoflondon.gov.uk/bunhillfields
Oct-Mar: 8am-4pm Mon-Fri; 9.30am-4pm Sat-Sun. Apr-Sep: 8am-7pm Mon-Fri; 9.30am-7pm Sat-Sun

Some 120,000 nonconformists, radicals and dissenters found a final resting place at the Grade I-listed Bunhill Fields. Though the cemetery closed to new burials in the mid-1850s, leftwing sympathisers continue to leave fresh flowers by the stones of William Blake, Daniel Defoe and John Bunyan, and enjoy the peaceful greenery of the adjacent gardens.

③ CURIOUS DUKE GALLERY

207 Whitecross St, EC1Y 8QP ☎ *7251 6551*
🖥 www.curiousdukegallery.com
11.30am-6.30pm Mon-Fri; noon-4pm Sat

Peppered with street art, Whitecross is already its own urban alfresco gallery. Curious Duke brings a little of this spirit indoors, supporting emerging contemporary artists and selling original prints.

④ HULA NAILS

203-205 Whitecross St, EC1Y 8QP
☎ *7253 4453* 🖥 *www.hulanails.com*
10.30am-7.30pm Mon-Tue;
10.30am-9pm Wed; 10.30am-7.30pm
Thur-Fri; 11am-6pm Sat

Electric pink walls, retro pin-up prints, intimate treatment rooms and a gentle tiki theme set this glamorous beauty salon apart from the rest. Therapists are dolled up like '50s starlets and can oblige with vintage-style hair and make-up, as well as everyday manicures, waxing and spray tans.

⑤ IRONMONGER ROW BATHS

1-11 Ironmonger Row, EC1V 3QF
☎ 3642 5520 ▭ www.better.org.uk
6.30am-9pm Mon-Fri; 9am-6pm Sat-Sun
Don't let the state-of-the art swimming pool,
gym and Turkish spa fool you: these public baths
have been at the heart of the local community
since 1931. The building underwent a major
renovation in 2012, and is now a sparkling blend
of heritage and modernity.

HOXTON

HACKNEY ROAD

HORATIO ST

Columbia Road

RAVENSCROFT STREET

JONES DAIRY CAFE

4

EZRA STREET

COLUMBIA ROAD

£4

2 3

ION SQUARE GARDENS

5

1

COLUMBIA ROAD

GOSSET STREET

SHOREDITCH HIGH STREET

COLUMBIA ROAD

Best known for its Sunday flower market, Columbia Road is a decidedly
weekend destination. Vendors start setting up in the early hours, and keen
shoppers arrive at 8am to snap up the freshest cut stems and pot plants, and
stock up on gardening equipment, seeds and sundries. By the market's close at
2pm, the vocal, friendly flower sellers are swiftly shifting bunches of blooms at
bargain prices, and the masses of people streaming between stalls are beginning
to thin. The bustling atmosphere remains all day, however, and the dinky shops
and cafés lining the road are usually heaving uncomfortably on Sundays.
If you don't fancy battling with prams, hipsters and tourists on market day,
your best bet is to visit on Saturday, when many of the shops are open.
Top draws include the fragrant Angela Flanders at number 96, an independent
perfumery which has been concocting intoxicating scents since 1985,
as well as Beyond Fabrics at number 67, where rolls of patterned cotton, baskets
of bobbins and every conceivable sewing implement are on offer.
For an afternoon snack, try Lily Vanilli's in the courtyard off Ezra Street –
the adventurous baker turns out fanciful creations, from cherry bakewell pies
to a divine pomegranate and coconut sponge.

① VINTAGE HEAVEN & CAKEHOLE

82 Columbia Rd, E2 7QB
🖥 *www.vintageheaven.co.uk*
Noon-6pm Sat; 8.30am-5.30pm Sun
Every surface and space of this family-run vintage store is piled high with antique china, Art Deco glassware, fancy cutlery and table linen. At the back, the cute Cakehole café serves homemade bakes and pots of tea.

② RYANTOWN

126 Columbia Rd, E2 7RG
☎ *7613 1510*
🖥 *www.misterrob.co.uk*
Noon-6pm Sat; 10am-4pm Sun
Perhaps the most twee of all the twee shops on Columbia Road, Ryantown showcases the much-loved work of British artist Rob Ryan. Among the paper-cut prints incorporating honey-sweet messages, you'll find Ryan's work printed on cushions, mugs, tote bags, ceramics and other gifts.

③ SUCK & CHEW

130 Columbia Rd, E2 7RG ☎ *8983 3504*
🖥 *www.suckandchew.co.uk*
Noon-4pm Sat; 9am-4.30pm Sun
Aniseed balls, cola pips, pear drops, gobstoppers, rhubarb and custards, sherbet lemons and many more are stored in glass jars and weighed out by hand in this traditional sweet shop.

④ JONES DAIRY

23 Ezra St, E2 7RH ☎ *7739 5372*
🖥 *www.jonesdairy.co.uk*
Shop: 8am-1pm Fri-Sat; 9am-2pm Sun
Café: 9am-3pm Fri; 9am-4.30pm Sat;
8am-3pm Sun
Tucked behind Columbia Road on a cobbled courtyard, Jones Dairy was a working dairy at the turn of the nineteenth century. Today, it sells farm-fresh produce, bread and artisan cheese, and serves up brunch and lunch in its rustic café.

⑤ HACKNEY CITY FARM

1a Goldsmiths Row, E2 8QA ☎ *7729 6381*
🖥 *www.hackneycityfarm.co.uk*
10am-4.30pm Tue-Sun
Urbanites can get acquainted with a host of farmyard animals, from donkeys and pigs to rabbits and guinea pigs, at this ramshackle, long-running city farm. The on-site, award-winning café is the perfect post-petting destination.

LONDON
FIELDS

WESTGATE STREET

1

2

3
4

BROADWAY MARKET

DUNCAN ROAD

F. COOKE LIVE EEL IMPORTER

REGENT'S ROW

BOAT

5

Broadway
Market

ANDREWS ROAD

PRITCHARD'S ROAD

BETHNAL
GREEN

BROADWAY MARKET

With Regent's Canal at one end, and London Fields at the other, Broadway Market is bookended by two of the East End's most popular alfresco haunts. The canal is a favourite with runners and cyclists, and a couple of moored barges open as book and bric-à-brac shops at the weekend. London Fields, meanwhile, encompasses a lido (originally opened in 1932 and restored in 2006), a playground and a snug pub. But the area's main attraction is the market itself. Established on a drovers' route to the City in the 1890s, but falling into decline in the 1980s, it was reintroduced by a troupe of proactive locals in the mid-noughties, rejuvenating the whole area in the process. Today, its food stalls pull in hordes of punters each Saturday, supporting the independent businesses that have popped up along the street. Look out for fishmongers Fin & Flounder and wonderful florist Rebel Rebel, as well as a couple of excellent bookshops, quaint fabric and haberdashery stores and sustenance stops including coffee favourite Climpson & Sons and slick gastropub Market Café. Among these fashionable services, you'll spy a few gentle reminders of Broadway Market's past. There's The Cat & Mutton at number 76 – a boozer which has been serving since the late 1600s, and F. Cooke at number 9 which has been dishing up pie, mash and eels since 1900.

① STELLA BLUNT
75 Broadway Market, E8 4PH
☎ 07958 716 916
12.30pm-6pm Wed-Fri;
10.30am-6pm Sat; noon-5pm Sun
Manoeuvre carefully through this tightly packed, two-floor store to avoid knocking into a host of immaculate kitsch crockery, reclaimed school chairs, Formica tables and thoughtfully chosen vintage curiosities.

② BROADWAY MARKET
Broadway Market, E8 4PH
🖳 www.broadwaymarket.co.uk
7.30am-6pm Sat
Join the mustachioed, tweed-wearing men and retro bike-wielding women filling their eco shopping bags with fresh produce, hot food, cakes, craft and fashion from around 100 sellers. At the top of the road, the smaller Netil Market (13-23 Westgate St, E8 3RL; 11am-6pm Sat) covers vintage threads, jewellery, homeware and yet more food.

③ L'EAU À LA BOUCHE
35-37 Broadway Market, E8 4PH
☎ 7923 0600
🖳 www.labouche.co.uk
8.30am-7pm Mon-Fri; 8.30am-5pm Sat;
9am-5pm Sun

This wonderfully fragrant French food store and deli makes room for a giant (and always busy) communal table, where diners munch on fresh salads, quiches and cakes. There's wine on barrel tap (locals enjoy a good-value carafe refill service), artisan cheese, store cupboard treats and farm produce.

④ THE FILM SHOP
33 Broadway Market, E8 4PH
☎ 7923 1230 📖 www.thefilmshop.co.uk
Noon-10pm Mon-Sun
Bucking the waning interest in local video rental stores, The Film Shop caters for movie fans with a penchant for international and independent cinema. The shelves are stacked with DVDs categorised by genre and filmmaker, so you can find that obscure Ingmar Bergman thriller with minimal fuss.

⑤ LOCK 7
129 Pritchard's Rd, E2 9AP ☎ 7739 3042
📖 www.lock-7.com
8am-6pm Mon-Sat; 10am-6pm Sun
While Lock 7's cycle workshop mechanics take care of your bike service, repair a puncture or tune your brakes, you can refuel with a Monmouth coffee and light lunch at the shop's waterside café.

LONDON
FIELDS

LAURISTON ROAD

5

OPEN
FOR
POTTERY
CARDS

VICTORIA PARK ROAD

4

VICTORIA PARK ROAD

Victoria Park
Village

LAURISTON ROAD

3

2

MORPETH ROAD

ROYAL
GATES

1

GORE ROAD

VICTORIA
PARK

VICTORIA PARK VILLAGE

Bordering the northwestern edge of Victoria Park, and at least half a mile from the nearest train station, this self-contained pocket of Hackney feels like a village plucked straight out of the British countryside. Its four main streets radiate outward from a central roundabout, which was transformed from a weed-ridden eyesore into a blooming, award-winning plot by resident gardener Caroline Bousfield. Her handiwork has given the village a much-loved centrepiece – but it isn't the only local award-winner. Wine shop Bottle Apostle and butchers The Ginger Pig have both won sought-after industry gongs, while gastropub The Empress has been decorated with a Michelin Bib Gourmand.

These destinations can be found alongside worthy neighbours, including fishmonger Jonathan Norris and the bustling Deli Downstairs, and a number of stellar pubs and restaurants. Tea and cake come via the homely Loafing; Vietnamese delights abound at Nāmo; and stone-baked pizza, a pint and a bit of live music are supplied at The Lauriston. It's worth remembering that the latter pub runs a 'pizza in the park service' on the weekends, taking phone orders and dropping off takeaways to loungers in the park.

① VICTORIA PARK
Best accessed via the Crown and Royal Gates on Grove Rd
www.towerhamlets.gov.uk
7am-dusk Mon-Sun

Overcrowded and polluted, the nineteenth-century East End was in dire need of green and open space. Queen Victoria backed plans for a pleasure garden, and Victoria Park (dubbed The People's Park) was developed in the 1840s. Over the decades its glamour faded, but a much-required facelift in 2012 has returned the park, monuments and boating lake to their former glory.

② HAUS
39 Morpeth Rd, E9 7LD ☎ 7536 9291
www.hauslondon.com
11am-6pm Thur-Sat; 11am-5pm Sun

Andrew and Jane Tye have filled their sleek store with a tasteful edit of contemporary design pieces for the home. Scandi-style furniture and creative lighting, kitchenware and gifts are sourced from international brands and indie designers.

③ THE GINGER PIG
99 Lauriston Rd, E9 7HJ ☎ 8986 6911
www.thegingerpig.co.uk
9am-6.30pm Wed-Fri; 9am-6pm Sat;
9am-3pm Sun

Handsome cooked meat pies eye you from the window of this legendary butcher shop. Its cuts of pork, beef and lamb are from animals reared free-range on the Yorkshire Moors, other meats are sourced responsibly, and the pies, pâtés and chutneys are all handmade.

④ VICTORIA PARK BOOKS
174 Victoria Park Rd, E9 7HD
☎ *8986 1124*
🖥 *www.victoriaparkbooks.co.uk*
10am-5.30pm Mon-Sun
If you can tear your kids away from The Toybox across the road, this children's bookshop is a real treasure. Jo and Cris De Guia make it their business to know what's new, what's being taught at school and what children – from tots to teens – are keen to read.

⑤ CAROLINE BOUSFIELD'S WORKSHOP
77A Lauriston Rd, E9 7HA ☎ *8986 9585*
🖥 *www.carolinebousfield.co.uk*
10.30am-5.30pm Tue-Wed & Fri-Sat
Potter (and gardener) Caroline Bousfield bought this old coach house back in 1975. She swiftly converted it into a workshop and has been busy behind the pottery wheel ever since. The space doubles up as a shop, with shelves piled high with glazed stoneware.

HOXTON
SQUARE

AIDA

Shoreditch

OLD
STREET

OLD STREET

OLD STREET

HACKNEY ROAD

③

CHARLOTTE ROAD

RIVINGTON STREET

CALVERT AVENUE

②

LABOUR AND WAIT

HOUSEHOLD
GOODS

LABOUR
AND
WAIT
OPEN

④

CURTAIN ROAD

SHOREDITCH HIGH STREET

①

LEONARD STREET

NEW INN YARD

REDCHURCH STREET

⑤

GREAT EASTERN STREET

BETHNAL GREEN ROAD

SHOREDITCH
HIGH
STREET

SHOREDITCH VILLAGE

Often described as London's creative hub, Shoreditch has seen a stream of big chain establishments trickle in over the last few years, diluting the area's once boho appeal and driving out some of the artists that sparked its gentrification in the late 1990s. Despite the cynical cool-chasers, however, an ever-burgeoning number of genuinely independent and imaginative retailers continue to maintain Shoreditch's villagey feel, and the streets entangled around Shoreditch High Street, Curtain Road and Great Eastern Street accommodate a hodgepodge of cult boutiques, vintage stores and dozens of dive bars, fashionable clubs and trendy pubs. The area's great heritage, however, ensures it's more than just a nightlife spot: Shoreditch Town Hall adds Victorian grandeur on Old Street, while the Church of St Leonard has been open for prayer since 1740. Its grounds have actually been a place of worship since the twelfth century; it was used as an actors' church in the 1500s and is also the resting place of James Burbage. An apt fact, given that the Elizabethan impresario built a playhouse (among the first in England) across the street where New Inn Yard meets Curtain Road.

① **LABOUR AND WAIT**
85 Redchurch St, E2 7DJ
☎ *7729 6253*
⌨ *www.labourand wait.co.uk*
11am-6pm Tue-Sun
A traditional hardware store with a fashionable twist, Labour and Wait has nostalgic, functional design down pat. Enamel jugs, wooden cleaning brushes, steel buckets and stylish screwdrivers should inspire you to inject a little chic into household chores.

② PAPER & CUP

18 Calvert Avenue, E2 7JP ☎ *7739 5358*
🖥 *www.paperandcup.co.uk*
8am-5pm Mon-Fri; 10am-5pm Sun
Individually selected, cheap-as-chips
secondhand books line the walls of this friendly
neighbourhood hangout – the rest of the
space is given over to a bright café. Enjoy both
in the knowledge that all proceeds go to the
Spitalfields Crypt Trust, a local charity which
supports people suffering homelessness
and addiction.

③ AIDA

133 Shoreditch High St, E1 6JE ☎ *7739 2811*
🖥 *www.aidashoreditch.co.uk*
10.30am-7pm Mon-Sat; noon-6pm Sun
It's typical for Shoreditch shops to offer
more than just one service, and Aida neatly
encapsulates the local trend. You can browse
rails of indie fashion for men and women, have
your hair fixed at the vintage beauty bar or stop
for a brew in its café.

④ THE PRINCE'S DRAWING SCHOOL

19-22 Charlotte Rd, EC2A 3SG
☎ *7613 8568*
💻 *www.princesdrawingschool.org*
9.30am-8.30pm Mon-Fri; 9.30am-5pm Sat
Founded by the Prince of Wales to champion
the discipline of drawing, this school
runs a public programme of evening and
daytime drawing classes, lectures and films.
There's also a gallery of student work on
the ground floor.

⑤ THE BOOK CLUB

100 Leonard St, EC2A 4RH ☎ *7684 8618*
💻 *www.wearetbc.com*
8am-midnight Mon-Wed;
8am-2am Thur-Fri; 10am-2am Sat;
10am-midnight Sun
There isn't anything this café-bar-club-
arts-venue doesn't do. You can pop in for
breakfast, roll up for late night drinking and
dancing, play a game of ping pong, book in
for a life-drawing class, or find a beau at
speed dating.

WEST

PADDINGTON CEMETERY

KINGSWOOD AVENUE

SALUSBURY ROAD

LONSDALE ROAD

QUEEN'S PARK

PUB DINING ROOM

HARVIST ROAD

BRONDESBURY ROAD

Queen's Park

QUEEN'S PARK

1
2
3
4
5

QUEEN'S PARK

Queen's Park grew furiously in the late nineteenth century: terraces sprung up to house the working classes, and its eponymous centrepiece – a 30-acre park designed in a figure of eight – was unveiled in honour of Queen Victoria's Golden Jubilee. The park quickly became the heart of the village, morphing with the changing needs of residents: a grandstand was installed in 1891, tennis courts in the '30s, allotments during WWII and an animal petting corner in the '90s. It continues to be well used and is justly celebrated each September on Queen's Park Day when village businesses set up stalls and local groups put on a show. The family festival is just one of the events organised by the voluntary Queen's Park Residents' Association, and joins the annual Open Gardens and Studios day in June and the Book Festival in May. Queen's Park Books on Salusbury Road has an integral role in the latter, encouraging celebrity and local authors to helm readings, talks and signings, while the neighbouring library and local schools get involved with children's events and workshops.

① MR FISH

51 Salusbury Rd, NW6 6NJ
☎ *7624 3555* 🖥 *www.mrfish.uk.com*
11am-midnight Mon-Sun

A local chippy with a London-wide reputation, Mr Fish looks like it's been transposed from a British seaside town. Its pleasantly retro décor is matched by a nostalgic menu (there's prawn cocktail to start and sponge pudding to finish), though the main draw is its freshly battered fish and light, crisp chips.

② IRIS

73 Salusbury Rd, NW6 6NJ
☎ *7372 1777* 🖥 *www.irisfashion.co.uk*
10am-6pm Mon-Wed; 10am-7pm Thur-Fri;
10am-6pm Sat; 10.30am-4.30pm Sun

Providing moneyed villagers (of which there are plenty) with high-end fashion, Iris stocks a discerning mix of labels in an airy, girly boutique. Chic threads by APC, Humanoid and Isabel Marant hang alongside a small collection of designer children's clothing.

3 THE SALUSBURY

50-52 Salusbury Rd, NW6 6NN
☎ *7328 3286*
🖥 *www.thesalusbury.co.uk*
5pm-11pm Mon; noon-11pm Tue-Wed;
noon-midnight Thur-Sat;
noon-11pm Sun

This bar and dining room has won a legion of fans with its convincing Italian menu and cosy pub interior, and it takes pride of place among three jointly owned and adjacent businesses that bear the name Salusbury. Pop next door for the Salusbury Wineshop (where you can try wines by the glass), or head two doors down for the Salusbury Foodstore – a fashionable deli and pizzeria.

❹ CC'S CAKE SHOP & NAMA

19 Lonsdale Rd, NW6 6RA
www.ccscakeshop.co.uk
/www.namafoods.com
9am-5pm Mon-Sun

Two contrasting businesses share the same open-plan premises here: sleek café Nama serves a virtuous and dedicated raw food menu featuring elaborate dishes such as vegan lasagna and (nut) cheese boards. The homely CC's, meanwhile, encompasses a bakery and cookery school which runs classes ranging from pastry making to sushi rolling.

⑤ QUEEN'S PARK FARMERS' MARKET
Salusbury Road Primary School,
Salusbury Rd, NW6 6RG
🖥 *www.lfm.org.uk*
10am-2pm Sun

Queen's Park residents flock to this award-winning market each Sunday, so be prepared to sidestep regulars gassing with friends if you want to cover some thirty stalls selling free-range and organic groceries, as well as more unusual products such as oak-smoked garlic.

BATH ROAD

FISHER'S LANE

CHISWICK COMMON

TURNHAM GREEN TERRACE

⑤

TURNHAM GREEN

THE OLD CINEMA
ANTIQUES

④

CHISWICK HIGH ROAD

Turnham Green

② ③

HEATHFIELD TERRACE

①

DUKE'S AVENUE

DEVONSHIRE ROAD

Chiswick House

Hogarth's House

TURNHAM GREEN

Though situated a little north of Chiswick's main attractions, Turnham Green has established itself as the commercial heart of the area. To its south runs an incredibly scenic stretch of the Thames dotted with rowing clubs and pubs for walkers. Inland, Palladian villa Chiswick House attracts vast numbers of tourists, as does Hogarth's House – the former country pad of Georgian artist William Hogarth. For Londoners, the rather upmarket Chiswick car boot sale operates on the first Sunday of every month from the school on Burlington Lane, and the area's centuries-old brewing heritage means there are plenty of historic pubs to enjoy. Frustratingly, there's little to get excited about along Chiswick High Road itself, dwarfed as it is by standard high street restaurants and chains, but offshoots Turnham Green Terrace and Devonshire Road lay claim to a stronghold of independent retailers. On Turnham Green Terrace, a number of delis have made the street a destination for fans of fine food, and Foubert's Café (a local institution since 1980) is famous for its Italian ice cream. Devonshire Road, meanwhile, offers clothes boutiques, gift shops and the ramshackle Strand Antiques at number 46.

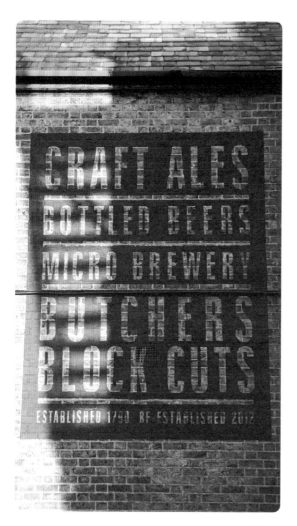

❶ THE LAMB BREWERY
9 Barley Mow Passage, W4 4PH
☎ *8994 1880*
🖥 *www.lambbrewery.co.uk*
11am-11pm Mon-Thur; 11am-1am
Fri-Sat; 11am-10.30pm Sun
This microbrewery, bar and dining room opened in 2012 in honour of the original Lamb Brewery that operated around the corner between 1790 and 1922. It brews eight craft beers and ales in its in-pub copper tanks, offering a more intimate alternative to a tour of nearby Fuller's Griffin Brewery, London's biggest independent beer maker.

❷ FOSTERS' BOOKSHOP
183 Chiswick High Rd, W4 2DR
☎ *8995 2768*
🖥 *www.fostersbookshop.co.uk*
10.30am-5.30pm Tue-Sat
The Foster family has run this tightly packed antiquarian store since 1968 and continues to acquire and sell a choice selection of rare books and first editions, together with volumes of local history and more general Penguin paperbacks and illustrated children's novels.

3 LA TROMPETTE

5-7 Devonshire Rd, W4 2EU ☎ *8747 1836*
🖳 *www.latrompette.co.uk*
Noon-2.30pm & 6.30pm-10.30pm
Mon-Sat; 12.30pm-3pm &
6.30pm-9.30pm Sun

La Trompette's Michelin star, refined décor and sophisticated French menu make it one of Chiswick's most prized neighbourhood restaurants. Owners Nigel Platts-Martin and Bruce Poole are also responsible for the superb Chez Bruce near Wandsworth Common and The Glasshouse in Kew, so you can be sure of a superlative dining experience.

4 THE OLD CINEMA

160 Chiswick High Rd, W4 1PR
☎ *8995 4166*
🖳 *www.theoldcinema.co.uk*
10am-6pm Mon-Sat; noon-5pm Sun

As its name implies, this antiques emporium was once a working picturehouse serving Chiswick locals in the early 1900s. Evidence of the building's original use survives, but the cavernous two-floor showroom is now crammed with attention-stealing homeware, ranging from opulent Art Deco dressers to polished steel factory furniture from the '50s.

5 TABARD THEATRE

2 Bath Rd, W4 1LW ☎ *8995 6035*
🖳 *www.tabardtheatre.co.uk*

A studio theatre with strong family appeal, this 96-seat fringe venue lives above nineteenth-century pub The Tabard. It may feel a little humble, but its in-house productions have been known to transfer to the West End and embark on UK tours. It also hosts regular comedy gigs.

HOGARTH'S HOUSE
open to the public

GUSTAV HOLST
composer
1874 – 1934
lived here
1908 – 1913

RIVER THAMES

LONSDALE ROAD

BARNES HIGHSTREET

CHURCH ROAD

BARNES COMMON

THE TERRACE

BARNES BRIDGE

ROCKS LANE

1

WHITE HART LANE

CROSS ST.

WESTFIELDS AVE.

3

2

Barnes

4

5

STATION ROAD

BARNES

BARNES VILLAGE

Of all London's Thameside villages, Barnes is perhaps the most alluring.
On any given day you'll see rowers powering down its snaking stretch of river,
locals making the most of a scenic promenade and families feeding the ducks
at the impossibly picturesque village pond. The Oxford-Cambridge Boat Race
in April is a yearly highlight here, though the community's willingness to
organise events mean there's always something worth pitching up for.
Barnes lays claim to one of the biggest summer fêtes in London, for example, as
well as an annual bonfire night and a weekly farmers' market.
There's an antiques fair on the first Saturday of every month and nightly live jazz
at the legendary music venue-cum-pub The Bull's Head on Lonsdale Road.
All this civic activity, coupled with an idyllic setting, keeps demand for houses
(and their prices) astronomically high. One of the most desirable spots is the
river-facing Terrace where Gustav Holst (composer of The Planets)
and Dame Ninette de Valois (founder of The Royal Ballet) once lived.
You can spy their Blue Plaques among other sights on the two-kilometre circular
Barnes Trail – just follow the metal markers embedded in the pavement.

1 ORANGE PEKOE

3 White Hart Lane, SW13 0PX ☎ *8876 6070*
🖥 *www.orangepekoeteas.com*
7.30am-5pm Mon-Fri; 9am-5pm Sat-Sun

This bright and airy tea room makes much of its expertly sourced loose-leaf tea stored strikingly in large black tins. An informal afternoon tea includes a blend of your choice, billowing scones and a decent wedge of cake, all served on vintage crockery.

2 TOBIAS AND THE ANGEL

68 White Hart Lane, SW13 0PZ ☎ *8878 8902*
🖥 *www.tobiasandtheangel.com*
10am-6pm Mon-Sat

It's not just the shop cat curled up on the sofa that makes Tobias and the Angel feel like home. Its creaky warren of rooms is furnished like a country house and shows off handcrafted furniture, vintage and new homeware, light shades, linens and hand-block-printed fabrics which are sold by the metre and used to make cushions, lavender bags and doorstops.

3 THE BROWN DOG

28 Cross St, SW13 0AP ☎ *8392 2200*
🖥 *www.thebrowndog.co.uk*
Noon-11.30pm Mon-Sun

Barnes Common dog walkers and their canines tend to decamp in this pooch-friendly pub where locally brewed cask ales are available on tap and bowls of water are dotted about on the floor. Ask the staff to snap a Polaroid photo of your pet and they may well add it to the doggy wall of fame.

4 THE OLYMPIC CINEMA

117-123 Church Rd, SW13 9HL
🖥 *www.olympiccinema.co.uk*

The Olympic Cinema opened in 2013, taking the place of the Olympic Sound Studios which famously played host to dozens of big names – The Rolling Stones, The Beatles, Queen, The Who and U2 among them – who recorded here over a forty-year period. The boutique cinema now incorporates a chic dining room, café and tuck shop.

5 LONDON WETLAND CENTRE

Queen Elizabeth's Walk, SW13 9WT
☎ *8409 4400* 🖥 *www.wwt.org.uk*
Nov-Mar: 9.30am-5pm Mon-Sat
Apr-Oct: 9.30am-6pm Mon-Sat

You'll see plenty of twitchers with flasks tucked under one arm and birdwatching guides under the other in this 105-acre Wildfowl and Wetlands Trust reserve. As well as a network of walkways and gardens, the centre offers an adventure playground, pond-dipping opportunities, an otter holt and guided tours.

MAIDA
VALE

RANDOLPH AVENUE

WARRINGTON CRESCENT

CLIFTON GARDENS

FORMOSA STREET

WARWICK
AVENUE

BRISTOL GARDENS

CLIFTON VILLAS

WARWICK AVENUE

BLOMFIELD ROAD

BLOMFIELD ROAD

BOAT

HARROW ROAD

Little
Venice

1
2
3
4
5

LITTLE VENICE

Little Venice – a triangular-shaped pool where the Grand Union Canal and Regent's Canal meet – is at the centre of a serene Paddington locale famous for its moored barges, leafy walkways and waterside pubs. Perversely, the evocatively named village couldn't feel less Italian, particularly when the annual Canalway Cavalcade bobs into town. Established in 1983, the very British festival sees more than 100 dressed-up boats gather on the water for a summer pageant, while Morris dancers and a real ale bar fuel the fun. At any time of year, however, it's normal to see bemused tourists intrigued by this countrified stretch of the city. To get a better feel for the area, it helps to wander off the waterway and explore Warwick Avenue's well-hidden village shops. A small section of Formosa Street is where you can unearth the majority of the retail activity and a number of genuinely good local eateries, though there are also a few boutiques along Bristol Gardens. Ramble beyond here and you'll be rewarded with spectacular local architecture which runs along majestic, tree-lined avenues. Make special note of the Italianate, mid-nineteenth-century housing on both Randolph Avenue and Warrington Crescent.

① HANDMADE INTERIORS
4 Formosa St, W9 1EE ☎ 7286 5100
🖳 *www.handmadeinteriorsshop.co.uk*
10am-6pm Mon-Fri; 11am-5pm Sat;
11am-4pm Sun

Textile and interior design duo Piyush Suri and Burcu Akin have taken inspiration from Turkish tiles and Scandinavian design symmetry to create a collection of screen-printed fabrics, soft furnishings and wallpapers. The pair sell their gorgeous pieces alongside homeware by other makers.

② THE PRINCE ALFRED & FORMOSA DINING ROOM
5A Formosa St, W9 1EE ☎ 7286 3287
🖳 *www.theprincealfred.com*
Noon-11pm Mon-Thur; noon-midnight
Fri-Sat; noon-10.30pm Sun

The Prince Alfred's original snug rooms, snob screens and decorative tiles make it one of the best examples of a late Victorian pub in London. The ornate bar is adjoined to the intimate Formosa Dining Room, which enjoys repeated recommendations in Michelin's *Eating out in Pubs* guide.

③ THE WATERWAY

54 Formosa St, W9 2JU ☎ *7266 3557*
🖳 *www.thewaterway.co.uk*
Noon-11pm Mon-Fri; 10.30am-11pm Sat;
11am-10.30pm Sun

The Waterway is fortunate enough to overlook the Grand Union Canal and its chief charm is a spacious outdoor terrace. Despite its alfresco allure, on a sunny day the restaurant-bar is up against stiff competition from the neighbouring Summerhouse (60 Blomfield Rd, W9 2PA), which is even closer to the water's edge.

④ CLIFTON NURSERIES

5A Clifton Villas, W9 2PH
☎ *7289 6851* 🖳 *www.clifton.co.uk*
Nov-Mar: 8.30am-5.30pm Mon-Sat
Apr-Oct: 9am-6pm Mon-Sat

Sandwiched between two houses on the residential Clifton Villas, this nursery has been incongruously located since 1851. It merits a visit even if you're not a garden owner, as its three interconnected shops stock pretty items for the home as well as garden-inspired gifts.

⑤ PUPPET THEATRE BARGE

Opposite 35 Blomfield Rd, W9 2PF ☎ 7249 6876

🖥 *www.puppetbarge.com*

This floating marionette theatre and local landmark opened back in 1982, and continues to present and tour productions for children and adults. If you don't have your sea legs, stick to dry land at the nearby Canal Café Theatre (Delamere Terrace, W2 6ND) which also programmes plays, comedy and cabaret.

GOLBORNE ROAD

Tourists often miss out on the delights of Golborne Road, unwittingly sticking to the main stretch of Portobello Road instead, and thanklessly battling with hordes of people who too have followed their guidebooks to the letter. Those who make their way toward the very north of Portobello Road will be rewarded with a far more casual shopping experience. Under the shadow of Ernö Goldfinger's infamous, 31-storey Trellick Tower, market sellers strew their jumble of bric-à-brac across rugs on the pavement, food stalls have space to offer seating, and shops range from secondhand furniture dens to contemporary gift stores. The substantial Moroccan, Lebanese and Portuguese communities here add an animated personality, as men sociably sip coffee in clamorous cafés and families eat freshly grilled fish served by Middle Eastern food vendors. It makes for a dynamic and intimate alternative to the more established and sprawling Portobello Road, though of course Golborne and Portobello are best visited together. Both areas share the same market days, with the majority of stalls open on Fridays, Saturdays and Sundays. Some traders work throughout the week, though mainly just the fruit and veg sellers.

1 UNITE & TYPE

341 Portobello Rd, W10 5SA
☎ *8964 4599*
💻 *www.uniteandtype.com*
10am-6pm Thur-Sat

A traditional printing press sits at the
back of this shop, ready for regular
in-store letterpress workshops.
The remaining space shows off printed
cards and playful mugs, bowls and
jugs made in a Staffordshire pottery.
If you're feeling creative, note that the
ceramics can be custom printed with
your own typography.

2 GEORGE'S PORTOBELLO FISH BAR

329 Portobello Rd, W10 5SA
☎ *8969 7895*
10.30am-11.30pm Mon-Fri;
10.30am-9pm Sat; noon-9.30pm Sun

George Periccos opened this fish and
chip shop in 1961 and you'll still find him
behind the counter making sure that fresh
cod, haddock and plaice is battered and
fried to his exacting standards. There's
limited seating, so be prepared to take
away – and to queue.

❸ T&F SLACK SHOEMAKERS
32B St Lawrence Terrace, W10 5SX
☎ *8969 9100*
🖳 *www.tandfslackshoemakers.com*
11am-6pm Mon-Fri; 10am-6pm Sat
Husband and wife duo Tim and Fiona Slack give classic British shoes a wickedly contemporary twist: there are brogues with bright soles, loafers stacked up on heels and Oxfords made from suede. By handcrafting the shoes in a London factory, they can also offer a custom service.

❹ JANE BOURVIS
89 Golborne Rd, W10 5NL ☎ *8964 5603*
🖳 *www.janebourvis.co.uk*
12.30pm-6pm Tue-Fri; 10.30am-5.30pm Sat
Walking into this vintage bridal shop feels like wandering into Miss Havisham's dressing room. Dozens of antique lace dresses hang from the ceiling, corsets weigh down rails, and every available surface is topped with trinkets, strings of pearls and wind-up music boxes.

❺ LISBOA PATISSERIE
57 Golborne Rd, W10 5NR ☎ *8968 5242*
7am-7.30pm Mon-Sat; 7am-7pm Sun
It's hard to believe anyone could find a more heavenly custard tart outside of Portugal than at Lisboa. The patisserie's legendary *pastéis de nata* are the reason that patient punters stand in line daily, though its *palmiers* and *pão de lietes* (milk bread rolls) are equally worth waiting for.

CLARENDON CROSS

Whether you're arriving at Clarendon Cross from Ladbroke Grove, or strolling up from Holland Park, you'll have the chance to admire rows of pastel-coloured houses lined up like Ladurée macarons in a box. These multimillion-pound properties were once the site of notorious slums known for their population of brick-makers and pig-keepers in the early 1800s and, later, impoverished and immigrant communities. Relics of the 'potteries and piggeries' era remain on Walmer Road where a tile kiln stands adjacent to the entrance of Avondale Park (itself once covered in pig slurry), and longtime residents still remember the area as infamously grotty right into the '60s. Clarendon Cross itself – a tiny spot with a big reputation – began life as a village of amenities in the early 1900s when there was a dairy and newsagent, a sweetshop and grocers. But the arty middle classes started arriving in the '70s, and the shops took on a more bohemian character. Gentrification took hold over the next twenty years and Clarendon Cross became a magnet for London's richest looking to raise their families in an attractive central locale. The mini village is now dominated by specialist homeware boutiques, and is a go-to destination for upmarket interior designers.

1 MYRIAD

131 Portland Rd, W11 4LW
☎ 7229 1709 🖳 www.myriad.me.uk
11am-6pm Tue-Thur & Sat

Sara Fenwick mixes antique finds from international markets with new stock and one-off commissions in this two-floor homeware store. Her style is casual luxury, so expect myriad farmhouse tables, bell jars, mirrors and battered leather armchairs.

② JULIE'S

135 Portland Rd, W11 4LW ☎ 7229 8331
🖳 www.juliesrestaurant.com
10am-3.30pm & 7pm-11pm Mon-Fri;
10am-4pm & 7pm-11pm Sat-Sun

When it opened in 1969, Julie's arguably put the then down-at-heel Clarendon Cross on the map. A-list actors, fashion royalty and rock 'n' roll legends once flocked here, and you might still see the odd star in one of the restaurant's many intimate, shabby-chic rooms and alcoves.

③ VIRGINIA

98 Portland Rd, W11 4LQ ☎ 7727 9908
11am-6pm Mon-Sat (ideally by appointment)
Clarendon Cross's concentration of eccentrics
and artists may be thinning these days, but long-
serving establishments such as Virginia keep the
area's unconventional personality alive. Virginia
Bates opened up shop in 1971 and is renowned
in the upper echelons of the fashion industry for
her incredible collection of antique apparel from
the 1850s to the 1930s.

④ THE TEMPLE GALLERY

6 Clarendon Cross, W11 4AP ☎ 7727 3809
🖳 *www.templegallery.com*
10am-5.30pm Mon-Fri (or by appointment)
Sir Richard Temple moved his Knightsbridge
gallery to this address in 1989, bringing with
him rare artefacts from the most niche of
genres: Russian icons and Byzantine antiquities.
An eminent expert on medieval sacred art,
Temple curates laudable temporary exhibitions
throughout the year.

⑤ THE CROSS

141 Portland Rd, W11 4LR ☎ *7727 6760*
🖥 *www.thecrossshop.co.uk*
10am–6pm Mon-Sat
The Cross was one of the first of its kind in London: a lifestyle boutique covering an inspiring blend of independent fashion labels, children's clothes, toys, gifts, accessories and jewellery. Every surface and rack of the shop's two floors is stuffed, making this a happily time-consuming place to visit.

INDEX

VILLAGES

BARS, PUBS & GASTROPUBS

CAFÉS & RESTAURANTS

MUSEUMS & GALLERIES

PUBLIC SPACES & VENUES

SHOPS

BEAUTY
Angela Flanders, 129
Floris, 45
Geo F. Trumper, 19
Hula Nails, 126
Verde London, 111
Whispers, 116

BOOKSHOPS
Daunt Books, 13
Fosters' Bookshop, 160
Paper & Cup, 147
Persephone, 30
Primrose Hill Books, 56
Queen's Park Books, 153
Review, 94
Victoria Park Books, 142

FASHION
Aida, 147
Annie's, 69
Atelier Mayer, 25
ChiChiRaRa, 87
De Roemer, 26
Felix & Lily's, 71
Fenton Walsh, 95
Fifi Wilson, 106
Iris, 154
Jane Bourvis, 178
Kooples, The 11

Leftovers, 101
North Cross Vintage, 87
Philip Treacy, 47
Scarlet Rage, 60
T&F Slack Shoemakers, 178
Virginia, 184
Whistles, 11

FOOD & DRINK
Bottle Apostle, 139
Cadenhead's Whisky Shop and
    Tasting Room, 11
Cannon & Cannon, 101
Cave, 42
Chelsea Fishmonger, 103
Cornercopia, 99
Deli Downstairs, 139
Dove, 110
Fin & Flounder, 135
Flock & Herd, 93
Franklin's Farm Shop, 90
Ginger Pig, The 139, 141
Hamish Johnston, 111
Haynes, Hanson & Clark, 103
Hive Honey Shop, The 111
Hope & Greenwood, 87
Jago Butchers, 103
Jane Asher Party Cakes &
    Sugar Craft, 107
Jeroboams, 45

Jonathan Norris, 139
Jones Dairy, 132
La Fromagerie, 11
MacFarlane's Deli, 119
Melange Chocolate Shop &
    Café, 97
Partridges, 55
Paul Rothe & Son, 14
People's Supermarket, The 30
Persepolis, 93
Philglass & Swiggot, 111
Pie Man, The 103
Salusbury Foodstore, 155
Salusbury Wineshop, 155
Shepherd Foods, 55
Suck & Chew, 132

HOMEWARE & GIFTS
Ben Pentreath, 30
Beyond Fabrics, 129
Button Queen, The 14
Caroline Bousfield's Workshop,
    142
Cave, 42
Chelsea Toys, 105
Circus, 101
Clifton Nurseries, 172
Colour Makes People Happy, 89
Conran Shop, 11
Cross, The 185

MARKETS

Frances Lincoln Limited
www.franceslincoln.com

London Villages
Copyright © Frances Lincoln 2013
Text copyright © Zena Alkayat 2013
Photographs copyright © Kim Lightbody 2013
Illustrated maps copyright © Jenny Seddon 2013
Designed by Becky Clarke

A catalogue record for this book is
available from the British Library.

ISBN 978-0-7112-3466-6
Printed and bound in China

9 8 7 6 5